The Gospel Stories of

Jesus

Sunday Bulletin Reflections for Year A

Matthew

By Deacon Dick Folger

The Gospel Stories of Jesus

Published by

2339 Davis Avenue
Hayward, CA 94545-1111, U.S.A.
510-887-5656
www.folgergraphics.com
E-mail: dickfolger@aol.com

Printed in the United States of America

Library of Congress Control Number 2001099249

ISBN 0-9715211-0-7

How others have used
The Gospel Stories of Jesus

The front page of our Sunday bulletin had been static for years. The front page just listed the Mass schedules, various parish phone numbers and other details.

In an effort to make the front page of the bulletin more readable, we began printing the Gospel story with an illustration and a short reflection. We sent the statistics to page two. People seemed to like the stories, so I kept writing and by the time we had printed the full three-year cycle, I had written 156 stories.

The Gospel Stories of Jesus were next published in Celebration, the worship resource of The National Catholic Reporter. This gave the stories a national audience and a much wider use.

Many churches began to print them in their Sunday bulletins. At a church in Baton Rouge, LA they even read one of the Gospel stories at Sunday Mass.

A Franciscan priest wrote to say he found the stories "extremely helpful for me as I prepare for my Sunday homily." Another reader said "I love to read them on Monday and walk with the story or image for the week."

A jail chaplain in California wrote to say, "I find them a wonderful way to share the Gospel story with the inmates in Saturday chapel."

Bible study groups have used the stories as "meeting starters" and youth ministers say the kids like to hear these "mini-movies" of the Gospels.

This book is copyrighted, but readers are welcome to reprint the stories in church bulletins and other materials as needed. No written permission is required, providing the following reference appears:
  "© *The Gospel Stories of Jesus by Deacon Dick Folger.*"

Jesus was a storyteller. And so we are all called to be storytellers for Jesus. In the closing words the Book of Matthew (28:19) we are commissioned: "Go then, to all peoples everywhere and make them my disciples!"

Deacon Dick Folger

Table of Contents

4

Illustrations in this book are taken from various sources. Many of the drawings are fine line wood engravings designed by the German artist Plockhorst. Some of the halftone illustrations were made by Heinrich Johann Michael Ferdinand Hoffman. Their works appeared in the 1895 edition of The Life of Christ by Hesba Stretton.Other art appeared in The Glories of the Catholic Church, 1894, Thomas Kelly, publisher. Still more came from the book Beautiful Pearls of Catholic Truth, 1930, New York Catholic Publishing Co. These books contained the work of H. S. Melville, P. Justyne. W. J. Allen, W. Thomas, Castelli, Makins, Lancelot, A. Sargent, Pearson, Harelay, W. J. Linton and Philip Poteau. Finally illustrations were taken from commercial clip art now in public domain.
Cover watercolor by Deacon Dick Folger

First Sunday of Advent
Matthew 24: 37-44

The Son of Man is coming

When Jesus mentioned Noah and the great flood, Peter's brother Andrew pretended to be paddling a boat. John, who was sitting next to him, stifled a laugh and covered his eyes with his hand. Peter snapped a glance at the two trouble-makers and then focused his glare on his younger brother. Andrew covered his face to regain composure.

Jesus continued: "So it will be at the coming of the Son of Man. Two men will be out in the field; one will be taken and one will be left."

Peter was momentarily tempted to point a finger at Andrew, indicating that if he wasn't careful he would be the one that would be left out in the field.

"The Son of Man is coming at the time you least expect," Jesus concluded.

Peter knew that he would be awake and alert, ready for the coming of the Son of Man. It might be any day now, he thought. But one example Jesus used had him concerned. Jesus said that Peter had to be prepared. Peter wasn't sure if he was properly prepared. One could stay awake and be alert, but why was one man left standing in the field while the other was taken. If the one that was left was unprepared in some way, then Peter had a problem. It was all pretty hard to understand and everyone was getting tired. The disciples had been listening to Jesus talk to them for most of the afternoon.

It had all begun earlier in Jerusalem when they had asked Jesus about the Great Temple. Philip wanted to know how such a magnificent structure could ever be destroyed. Jesus had told them that not one stone would be left upon the other. As they walked along the explanation led them to try to understand the end time and the coming of the Son of Man.

Now the disciples were gathered around Jesus looking out across the Kidron Valley from the Mount of Olives. The temple was prominent above the wall of the city. The sun was getting low in the sky and Jerusalem was turning gold in the softer light.

Peter heard his stomach growl. The heady teachings of the afternoon were soon forgotten as his hunger took over and urgent plans for the evening meal were made.

✝

Jesus told the disciples that because Noah was prepared he was saved. The homeowner who was on watch for thieves was not robbed. But of the men and women in the field and grinding meal only two were saved. The other two were left behind. All four of these people may have expected the coming, but only two were truly prepared by doing and living out the will of God. As we move into the season of Advent we know that Christmas is coming. What remains for us is to truly prepare for it by doing and living out the will of God in our lives.

2nd Sunday of Advent
Matthew 3: 1-12.

Vipers!

John the Baptist sat alone on the large boulder at the edge of the Jordan River. With his eyes closed his mind raced with thoughts and ideas which were his communion with God. In this busy contemplation his whole morning had rushed by with only the sound of the river current gurgling over rocky shallows.

The desert solitude ended abruptly with voices rising beyond the western bank. With serpentine grace, John slid from the boulder to the water, sinking up to his waist. Holding his arms up, like wings, he waded across to meet whoever was coming. In moments John was engulfed by a crowd of noisy men who had come down seeking his baptism.

Most seemed to be common workers from the villages and hills. Some may have come down from Jerusalem, especially the five well-dressed Sadducee priests. Walking near these priests were a few older men who probably were conservative Pharisees. John was disturbed by their presence. In their orthodoxy they refused to believe in the Messiah, living only the letter of the law but ignoring the spirit.

Looking like a madman, John stalked toward them through the knee-deep water. He jabbed his finger in their direction and erupted in a fierce voice: "You brood of vipers!" Like a long whip, the words snapped over their heads, making them duck down for protection. John was out of the water and moving rapidly toward them as others backed away. "Who told you to flee from the wrath to come? Give some evidence that you mean to reform!"

"We are the sons of Abraham," one offered in defense.

John squatted down and picked a handful of small rocks from the river bed. One of the Pharisees, expecting a hail of stones, repositioned himself behind the others.

"Don't pride yourselves on the claim, "Abraham is our father.' I tell you, God can raise up children to Abraham from these very stones." John held out his hand and let the little rocks cascade to the ground.

Every eye was fixed on John. Captivated by his power, they were eager for the cool water that would wash them and cover them with the protective covenant of God.

✞

The Gospel Story of John's riverside encounter with the Sadducees and Pharisees challenges us to examine our own level of faith. Do we just do enough to get by? Is our faith just a prayer shawl we "put on" for Sunday morning? Our call to fruitful Christian lives means we must carry our faith out of the front door of the church and into Monday, Tuesday and the rest of the week.

3rd Sunday of Advent
Matthew 11: 2-11

A message for John

John the Baptist sat in the dim light staring at the metal bars of his prison cell. As the pungent odors trapped in the airless cellar burned in his nostrils, John closed his eyes and escaped to the sunlight of the desert where a clean, hot wind was blowing across his face.

High above John's prison cell, on the terraces of the castle, a cool breeze flowed through Salome's dark hair. It made her smile with pleasure. Her eyes darted briefly to meet a return glance from Herod Antipas, who sat clutching his wine goblet with one fat hand, the other sprawled on the thigh of his new wife, Herodias.

In the silence of his cell John continued to struggle with dark doubts about Jesus. Despite the unforgettable memories of their meeting—the baptism, the voice in the heavens—John still wondered. Who was this man? Perhaps one day his answer would come back from the messenger he had sent to see Jesus.

The clank of keys announced the approach of a prison guard. John stood and took two steps to the cell entrance and pressed his shaggy face against the bars. It was Aurius, the young guard who a week before had looked the other way when a visitor had managed to get to John.

"Someone's coming," Aurius said without breaking stride as he passed John's cell. In a moment the messenger was at John's door. "I saw Jesus," he reported.

"What did he say?" John urged.

"Jesus said to tell you what I hear and see:—that blind men see, cripples walk, lepers are made clean, the ears of the deaf are opened and dead men have been raised to life."

His messenger left quickly, leaving John with a smuggled piece of bread. As he chewed, the impact of the message wrenched tears from John's eyes. These were the words of the Prophet Isaiah which Jesus knew John would recognize as a special sign. Suddenly all doubts flowed away, leaving the baptizer filled with a warm glow of peace. There was no question. Jesus really was the messiah, the one to come.

When Aurius and other guards came for him a few moments later, John was smiling. Even as he bowed before the headsman, his heart still sang in the peace of Christ. John had been privileged to be the herald in the desert—the first to call Jesus 'The Lamb of God.'

Later, on the terrace, Herodias thought the expression on John's face was a grimace. She could never know that it was John's triumphant smile.

✚

Like John the Baptist, we are all subject to dark nights of doubt. But, like the dawn, Jesus sends the bright message that calms our hearts. Jesus is the Lamb of God who takes away the sins of the world. Jesus is born again each day in the hearts of those who love him.

4th Sunday of Advent
Matthew 1: 18-24

And you shall name him Jesus

The sullen skies darkened over the town of Nazareth and it looked like a morning rain was coming. Joseph peered up at the clouds and ducked inside his little shop.

He opened the shutters and soft light spilled over his familiar tools and tables. There was a feeling of peacefulness and safety in his predictable routine. Here he could try to make some sense of all that was happening to him. In his shop Joseph could lose himself in work and not have to face the realities of Mary and last night's frightening visions.

Joseph picked up a timber he was shaping and locked it in place with wedges. He began to chop and scrape against the wood with his sharp adze. Shavings of wood sliced away and dropped in curls at his feet.

The news that Mary was pregnant had crushed Joseph. As he cut, he raged over the insult and humiliation that Mary had been intimate with someone else while betrothed to him. Thoughts of writing a divorce paper would mean confronting the embarrassing family arrangements, both financial and emotional. Joseph's honor and life were ruined. What had once been his love for Mary was changing into hatred.

In addition to his heartache over Mary, Joseph now faced the enormous problem of last night's visions. He'd awakened to a room filled with light. Thinking it was morning, Joseph tried to get out of bed and came face to face with someone floating in front of him. The bright figure was in the air, smiling down at him. Joseph stared in disbelief.

Then the angel figure's unspoken words sprang clearly into Joseph's ears: "Joseph, descendant of David, do not be afraid to take Mary as your wife. For it is by the Holy Spirit that she has conceived."

Like a madman, terror went crashing through Joseph's mind. He tried to flee, thrashing in his blankets as the angel figure continued to smile.

The angel's eyes spoke again: "She will have a son and you will name him Jesus—because he will save his people from their sins."

This time Joseph lurched to his feet, his blankets falling away as the strange light dissolved into darkness. Breathing hard, Joseph groped his way outside and stood under the starless sky. It had all been too real to be a dream.

Joseph was cutting too deeply into the timber. He stopped. Mary's sweet face rose in his memory and Joseph realized she could never have dishonored him. The message from the angel must be true!

Putting his adze aside, he dropped the window shutter on his shop and stepped outside into the light rain. He began to walk in the direction of Mary's house.

As he went, Joseph bolstered his resolve, "I will believe that it is by the Holy Spirit that she has conceived. I place myself in Yahweh's care." Eagerly, he hurried to her. The rain was coming harder.

Mary was standing in her doorway when she saw him. With a soaring heart she ran up the rocky path. They embraced, standing a long time in the rain. A roll of thunder sounded in the mountains.

Little Mary looked up at Joseph and whispered, "You will name him Jesus." It was Joseph's final assurance that the dream was real. Mary's face was all wet and between them they were holding God in their love. Overwhelmed, Joseph's tears ran unnoticed with the rain.

✞

The test of our faith comes when, like Joseph, we are able to follow God against all earthly reasons. By taking Mary, Joseph faced ridicule from his family, friends and neighbors. Only his faith in God could give him assurance that Mary was a virgin. It is an inspiring image of strength and faith as we see the future earthly father of Jesus choose to follow God despite everything.

Christmas
Luke 2: 15-20

The happiest night of the World

When the night sky began to streak with light, nine-year old Aachim scrambled on his hands and knees toward his sleeping flock. In the growing light the terrified shepherd boy huddled next to *Old Moto* as if his favorite sheep could protect him.

The dome of night looked like a pitcher of goatsmilk was being poured into its bowl. The whiteness spread like wispy clouds driven on strong wind. The pale light thickened and began forming into the shape of a woman with outstretched arms. Suddenly the milk-light snapped to life and an angel floated above Aachim. Her brilliant white robes billowed about her.

Aachim pressed harder against *Old Moto,* his eyes fixed on the vision above him. The angel was young and her face was beautiful. Her eyes brightened when she smiled at him. In that moment Aachim realized there were now hundreds of angels filling the sky. Softly at first, but growing louder, their voices began to sing out "Glory to God." The chorus filled the sky and poured over the hills like soft rain.

The angel spoke to Aachim, saying "You have nothing to fear. I come to proclaim good news to you! I am bringing you tidings of great joy to be shared by the whole people. This day in David's City a savior has been born to you, the Messiah, and Lord. Let this be a sign to you: in a manger you will find an infant wrapped in swaddling clothes."

In the light from the skies Aachim could see all the way down the hills toward Beth Lehem where the tent of his family was pitched. Leaving the sheep behind he ran, almost stumbling, down to his tent. By the time he reached the tent the angels had dissolved back into the starry night sky. Aachim's mother and father were already up, standing in front of the tent looking up at the stars. One star burned as bright as the moon and together the little family walked in its direction.

A crowd of shepherds had already gathered at the entrance to the animal manger behind Beth Lehem's inn. Aachim and his parents worked their way to the front of the crowd to see. Just as the angel had said, there was a woman holding a newborn baby. Their faces were golden in the flickering torch light. Aachim heard one of the shepherds share what he had learned. "They are Joseph and Mary from Nazareth. The child's name is Jesus."

They all stood staring at the scene. It was just as the angel had told them. Aachim wondered what the angel's strange words meant when she said this child was to be a savior, a messiah?

Aachim felt his mother's hands gently rest upon his shoulders. He looked up into her brimming eyes and saw the forming tears. A warm breeze caressed them as they stood helplessly in awe and wonder.

✟

Each Christmas the world stands helplessly in awe and wonder among the shepherds who came to the manger on that first night. To wonder at the ways of God who chooses to be born unto us as a little baby. To marvel that God loves us enough to live and walk among us-a God who would die for us.

In this child is the great gift of eternal life. What more could we ask? It truly is the "Happiest Night of the World!"

The Holy Family
Matthew 2: 13-15, 19-23

The flight into Egypt

Joseph lay awake, staring out at the starry night sky. The days he'd just experienced had been overwhelming. First, finding a place in Bethlehem, then the birth of Jesus. All day the crowds of shepherds and villagers had come to see the newborn child. Then, just hours ago, the three great kings who had brought gifts for Jesus.

Joseph reached out to make sure the heavy bag of coins was still safe beside him. It was more gold than he had ever seen. Little corners of anxiety began to worry him and Joseph knew he must be very strong to protect Mary and Jesus and all these valuable gifts. Many men had seen the gifts and knew he now had them. In the morning they would leave quietly and start back for Nazareth. Joseph nodded and fell into a fitful sleep.

Mary woke when Joseph's arm came crashing down on her shoulder. Joseph was dreaming and was shielding his eyes against the bright light. Squinting he saw that the light was resolving itself into the form of an angel. She was stunning—clear and pure and beautiful. The words she spoke came like music, swelling in ever louder waves and sounding within him.

"Get up," the music words commanded, "take the child and his mother, and flee to Egypt. Stay there until I tell you otherwise. Herod is searching for the child to destroy him."

Joseph was sitting upright when he opened his eyes to the dark of the stable. The angel was gone. The vision and thc music left him trembling.

"I must be strong," he told himself, getting his feet beneath him. Joseph placed his hand gently on Mary's shoulder. She awoke immediately.

"What?" she asked.

"Come," Joseph said, "we must leave for Egypt!"

"Now, in the middle of the night?" Mary asked.

"Yes, the Angel said that Herod was trying to destroy Jesus."

"What Angel?" she asked, brushing her hair away from her young face.

"Mary, we must hurry, I'll tell you about it on the way."

Without a word, Mary gathered her things into the bag and took Jesus gently into her arms. She moved to the entrance of the stable and looked fearfully out at the dark hills. A chill of cold ran through her and she adjusted the blankets around Jesus to make sure he would be warm enough.

Joseph led the donkey out and tied their belongings down to the straps girding the animal.

"Do you want to ride?" Joseph asked.

"No," Mary said, "we'll walk awhile. Which way is it to Egypt?"

"South. We will find safety in the south." Joseph declared, his eyes full of courage and love.

✞

Sometimes in our lives the angel of invitation may appear, calling us to get up and go in an unexpected direction. Joseph's great faith enabled him to take his family and leave immediately for a place he'd never been. Jesus invited his future disciples to interrupt their lives and leave immediately. In the same way he comes in today's Gospel and he invites us to get up and follow him.

Epiphany
Matthew 2: 1-12

The Epiphany
of the Lord

THE PALACE GUARDS opened the gates for the three Persian rulers. The kings walked briskly under the Roman arch and out into the streets of Jerusalem. Sunlight brightened their colorful robes as they paused to look back.

Above, on the portico, Herod Antipas looked down on them, raising his hand in silent farewell. Herod closed his hand leaving his forefinger extended as a silent warning not to forget his directions to gather information about this "newborn king." Gaspar, Melchior and Balthazar nodded their heads respectfully to their host. They would return soon to "report their findings to him." Herod, the Tetrarch of Galilee watched his guests walk in the direction of the Jaffa Gate.

Outside Jerusalem the kings mounted the waiting camels and headed toward the Bethlehem hills. In the darkness of night they would continue to follow the star that had brought them to this distant land. There they would see the prophecy that had already been fulfilled. They would be among the first to worship the newborn king. They would bring him gifts of gold, frankincense and myrhh to sustain the Holy Family in their flight to Egypt.

Later that night, the kings camped within sight of the stable where Jesus lay. As they slept atop their royal robes they were filled with a vivid dream. A beautiful angel appeared to them. Her bright eyes and luminous skin were lit with unearthly light. She smiled and spoke in a voice that was like the music of tinkling bells fluttering like leaves in a breeze. "Do not return to Herod," she said.

At sunrise, Gaspar, Melchior and Balthazar packed up and rode out atop their camels. Heading home to Persia they rode silently, remembering

the vision of Jesus and the angel in their dreams. The morning sun lifted off the hills to the east and warmed their faces. After a time the kings reined their camels to a stop. Looking back they saw Bethlehem's buildings were now only a smudge of gold on the sunlit hillside. Beyond Bethlehem they could no longer see the lofty heights of distant Jerusalem.

✟

We are all like the wise men, the astrologers, the magi, the three kings. We seek to find the same thing. We search for the Newborn King in our own lives. We, too, follow the star, the light that beckons, the light that invites us to faith. We bring the gifts of our love, our time and our talent, presenting them to Jesus, the king of our lives. And, like Gaspar, Melchior and Balthazar, we must have the courage to turn our back on the Herods of our world, returning to our faith by any possible route.

The Baptism of the Lord
Matthew 3: 13-17

The Baptism of the Lord

John the Baptist put his right hand on the back of Jesus' neck and gripped Jesus' arm with his other hand.

"Just lean back with me. I will guide you," John said as he eased Jesus backwards into the waist-deep water.

Jesus gasped as the cold water claimed him, flooding the warmth of his back and gushing up around his shoulders. As his head went underwater, Jesus held his breath and scrunched his eyes tightly shut. He could feel the current flowing past him. Floating just below the surface in the watery silence, Jesus felt peace come over him.

John held Jesus firmly, pushing him down into the Jordan. Through the rippling water, Jesus' face was framed with the dark crown of his swirling hair. John saw Jesus' tranquil expression, like that of a sleeping child. He wasn't struggling for air like most of the people John baptized.

The words of Isaiah and Ezekiel flowed into Jesus' mind; words about God's spirit being poured out like water, cleansing and empowering. John the Baptist was preaching that the baptism and repentance required of non-Jews now was necessary for everyone, even the Jews themselves. And John was truly a prophet. And Jesus had come to fulfill the prophecy.

Jesus' eyes burst open underwater, startling John. His eyes remained fixed on something in the sky as he stood up in the water. John backed away to behold Jesus, water streaming down his uplifted face.

Jesus saw the sky split open and fill with warmth and light. The shimmering light began to take a shape, forming itself into a white blur that suddenly resolved into a beautiful dove. Its wings opened and it began to descend toward Jesus, sending light rays shining down before it.

Jesus was overwhelmed with the presence of God filling the dove and overflowing into a Spirit which charged the air with electricity and then the scent of flowers.

A great voice spoke words that thundered across the skies and up the

mountainsides; and out across the desert waste; and into every part of Jesus mind. They were words seemingly as immense as centuries of time—words encompassing all languages, words becoming all the sounds of the universe. All of this distilled itself into a tiny whisper which only Jesus could hear: "You are my beloved Son. On you my favor rests."

✟

In celebrating the Baptism of Jesus this Sunday, we also celebrate our own baptism—our rising up from the water to receive new life. We celebrate that we became Children of God. We celebrate our Confirmation when we received the Holy Spirit. We celebrate the gift of Communion as we share in the banquet of Christ's sacrifice. We celebrate our life, living as Christians so that in our dying we receive Eternal Life.

Second Sunday in Ordinary Time
John 1: 29-34

The Lamb of God

John the Baptist had come up from the Jordan River through the oasis city of Jericho. He marched up the mountain road that climbed to Bethany, the town where Jesus was visiting.

Bethany perched on the southeastern side of the Mount of Olives. Jerusalem was less than two miles distant. The Bethany Road led around the side of the mountain to reveal a magnificent view of the great city, rising up from cliffs across the Kidron Valley.

Bethany was the home of Jesus' friends, Martha, Mary and Lazarus and one day it would witness the great miracle of the raising of Lazarus from the dead.

Bethany was also the home of Simon the Leper where in time Jesus would be anointed with the sweet perfumes that foretold his death; and from which he would depart for a triumphant ride through cheering throngs into Jerusalem.

But this day Jesus was not yet to be known. He was just a 30-year-old carpenter's son, down from Nazareth, to visit Martha, Mary and Lazarus.

The afternoon heat drove several of the old men of the village to the shade of a house. Sitting on the ground and leaning back against the wall, they waited silently for the afternoon breeze. Instead they got a stranger. He was a wild-looking man hiking up the road.

John the Baptist was glad to have finally arrived in Bethany for a chance to rest and drink before continuing. When he arrived John saw the old men sitting in the shade.

"Mind if I join you?" he asked. No one moved or answered so John sat down next to them. He sighed and closed his eyes for a moment.

When John opened his eyes again he squinted into the blaze of sunlight, and was startled to see Jesus walking toward him. John struggled to his feet and pointing toward Jesus exclaimed: "Look! There is the Lamb of God! It is Jesus who takes away the sin of the world!"

The old men only saw the carpenter's son and began to clear their throats in embarrassment. Their questioning looks confirmed that they thought John must be deranged. The baptizer tried to tell them that he had seen the Spirit descend like a dove from the sky, and that it had come to rest on Jesus.

The old men's eyes twinkled as they patiently listened to John's incredible story.

Jesus greeted John and stepped into the shade. The old men looked up at the two young men. It would be still be a long time before they would come to know the truth.

A merciful breeze finally arrived and the heavy air began to move.

✞

Until we recognize Jesus in our lives, we are like the village men of Bethany. Sometimes we may need a modern-day John the Baptist to point out the presence of Jesus in our lives. We may be so busy and so preoccupied that we have failed to see him in our midst. The timeless words of the Gospel speak to us this day: "When you see the Spirit descend and rest on someone, it is he who is to baptize with the Holy Spirit." If we look, we can see the working of the Holy Spirit in our midst as God uses each and every one of us to be the love he has for us.

Third Sunday in Ordinary Time
Matthew 4: 12-23

Day of decision

The afternoon sun was slowly baking the day. Jesus waded out into the cool water. The sparkling Sea of Galilee sprawled southward. Behind Jesus was the city of Capernaum which was busy about its business of fishing, farming and trade. As Jesus cooled his feet, he reflected on the turbulent events which had brought him here.

The water of the lake was the same water that had flowed in the Jordan River where John had baptized him. Jesus remembered the day of his baptism—John the prophet with eyes ablaze, the dove and the thunderous voice they had heard above them.

The authority in the voice in the heavens was echoed in John's prophecy. The Baptist was not afraid to declare the truth and even to speak out against the most powerful man in his world, the Tetrarch of Galilee, Herod Antipas. The example of John's great courage and powerful preaching inspired Jesus. But the price of John's preaching was prison. The news that Herod had siezed John and thrown him in the castle dungeon filled Jesus with anguish.

After John's capture, as Jesus trudged back to his home in Nazareth, he had plenty of time to reflect. Jesus sensed a curious feeling that his own life was a reflection of John's— that he would also face prison and death if he dared to speak out. Yet Jesus also knew that the time had come when he must be the One foretold by John. The time had come when Jesus must begin his ministry.

The first hint of breeze came in off the lake and Jesus waded back to the shore. He sat down on a flat rock and began to examine his newly washed feet. The bitter memory of Nazareth assailed him. Jesus disastrous declaration that he was the fulfillment of the scripture had been rejected by the townspeople in the synagogue. But the scripture from Isaiah the Prophet

A.L. Rawson

had clearly read: "…the people from the land of Zebulun and Naphtali would no longer walk in darkness—they would see a great light." Nazareth was in Zebulun and Capernaum was in Naphtali.

Jesus sat on the rock a long time. When he rose his face was bright with new resolve. He would enjoy this last night alone. In the morning he would begin to seek out his disciples one by one among the fishermen on this very shore.

✟

When we make our decision to be disciples of Jesus we find that discipleship begins in a humble way right where we are, on our own shore. We, like Jesus, must have the conviction and courage to claim the practice of our faith one step at a time as we journey on the road of our life day by day.

Fourth Sunday in Ordinary Time
Matthew 5, 1-12

Blessed are you...

As Jesus picked his way down the hillside trail his mind was already filling with what he was going to say. He looked our across the lake and felt the breeze on his face. It lifted his hair away from the sides of his face and felt soothing in the afternoon heat. The sun was now at his back and his shadow pointed ahead of him, a black arrow on the golden grass. Jesus walked toward a grove of tall eucalyptus trees standing on a plateau overlooking the sea. A large crowd was waiting for him under the shade beneath the chattering leaves of the wind-brushed trees.

When Jesus drew closer he noticed many people spilling out from the crowd onto the plateau beyond the grove. Their voices grew louder with recognition as Jesus approached. Silence settled as he moved among them and then further down the hill. They followed with the sun on their backs. The vast throng filled the bowl-shaped hillside making it a perfect amphitheater. Jesus motioned for them to be seated and as they settled he noticed his disciples taking front-row positions.

Facing into the sunlight, Jesus raised his arms and said: "Blessed are you poor; the reign of God is yours."

The words were like warm oil poured out on dry, cracked feet. Each one who heard Jesus words knew the yoke of Rome and the rule of Herod. These gathered people knew the bite of their tax collectors. They were the poor. They suffered the harshness of the land and the emptiness of the sea.

Some were poor in spirit, trapped in an emotional bog from which there seemed no escape.

Jesus next spoke of the sorrowing, the lowly and those who thirsted for holiness. Jesus words engulfed them like a cold, freshwater stream bursting up from the desolate desert. For the merciful, the peacemakers and the persecuted Jesus was reason to rejoice and be glad. The people who had walked in darkness had indeed seen a great light!

H. Hoffman

✝

When Jesus preached the Beatitudes he gave us his personal assurance that everything is going to be okay. He said "I'm going to take care of you." He said, "Hush now, don't you cry." He invites us to really believe and live by his closing words: "Be glad and rejoice, for your reward in heaven is great!" Jesus also challenges us with his way of life. He invites us to make the reign of God present in our lives by being lowly, hungering for justice, showing mercy and making peace.

Fifth Sunday in Ordinary Time
Matthew 5: 13-16

Light!

The smell of roasting lamb mixed with the sharp scent of smoke that floated out from the fire. Jesus and his followers encircled the roasting pit in the backyard at Peter's house in Capernaum. It was taking longer than expected and evening was turning to night. In the east the sky was dark enough for the brightest stars to appear. Over the dark surface of the lake the hush of night had fallen and the last few scattered breezes hurried shoreward.

Jesus surveyed the hungry faces of his new followers. Their eyes were bright, reflecting an orange glint from the dancing fire.

They had been talking about salt losing its power and then having no value for flavor or even as catalyst to fuel a fire. The firelight reminded Jesus that the value of each one's life was like the dance of the flames. Their lives give warmth and light. They consume and become energy. Then Jesus thought about his own life and how the flames of it give a warmth and light that must be felt and seen in order to fulfill God's plan.

A strange urgency overcame Jesus as he thought about his *Father's plan*. Thirty years of quiet living were behind Jesus and now it was beyond time to him to fulfill the scriptures. He, himself, would become the light of the world. It was time to let his light shine beyond the towns of Galilee's shore.

One of the disciples, interrupting Jesus' thoughts. was still thinking about salt. He pinched up a few granules and tasted them. "This is good salt." He sprinkled some on the roasting lamb as he turned the skewer. "It looks like we're ready to eat!"

Jesus watched him lift the meat from the fire. "It's not the flavor of salt that's important. It's the fire of your lives and how you live them."

One of them said: "How should we live?"

Jesus answered: "You are the light of the world. A city set on a hill cannot be hidden. Men do not light a lamp and then put it under a bushel

W.J. Linton

basket. They set it on a stand where it gives light to all in the house. In the same way, your light must shine before all so that they may see goodness in your acts and give praise to your heavenly Father."

As Jesus spoke these words he realized he could no longer hide his own light under a bushel basket. He must become the city on a hill.—a light that would shine before all.

✞

As Jesus preached these words that night, he preaches them this Sunday to each of us. Perhaps, like Jesus, we have lived a long lifetime in quiet, keeping our light hidden under a bushel basket. Jesus invites us to uncover our light. He asks that we put it on a stand where our light can shine for all. When others see the goodness of our acts it becomes praise to our heavenly Father.

Sixth Sunday in Ordinary Time:
Mt. 5: 17-37

'I have come to fulfill them...'

The crowds gathered on the hillside had never heard anyone like Jesus before. His confident words were like pure scripture. To these Galileeans it was as if Yahweh himself was speaking to them. Jesus had been quoting scripture from the book of Deuteronomy, but his own words seemed more sacred.

Jesus' teachings were like the masterful toss of a huge fishing net. He would cast his concept out above the crowd, letting it slowly settle over them. As they understood his words they were captivated and filled with a strange excitement.

Jesus said he wasn't trying to replace the Jewish laws. He said he was bringing these laws to refinement and perfection.

Jesus opened his arms in welcome and proclaimed: "I have come, not to abolish the law and the prophets. I have come to fulfill them!"

He told them the laws weren't about just getting by and doing the minimum. He invited them to embrace the law completely. To let it seep beneath their skin and into their lives.

The people came to understand that it is the seemingly smaller sin of anger which leads to the grave sin of murder. It is the seemingly smaller sin of lustful thoughts which lead to the serious sin of adultery. Adultery leads to divorce. Oaths and agreements are made to be broken unless they flow from an honest and truthful heart.

Jesus told them: "Say *yes* when you mean *yes* and *no* when you mean *no*. Anything beyond that is from the evil one."

✞

Today we are still called to fulfill the laws which Jesus preached about on the hillside near Capernaum. We are still told that we are called to follow not only the big laws, but even the smallest of these commands.

We are challenged to obey the spirit of the law as well as the specific words. If murder is against the law, aren't the seeds of anger also? Isn't the lustful glance or the little white lie the source of a greater evil?

Jesus says that "getting by" is not enough. As we approach the Lenten season Jesus teachings in this Sunday's Gospel gently lead us to a more profound preparation.

1st Sunday of Lent
Matthew 4: 1-11

'Not on bread alone...'

Jesus was drifting in and out of consciousness. The cave was like a tomb and Jesus was a skeleton inside it. His paper-thin skin was raw from the cruel rocks. Jesus had been fasting in the desert for nearly six weeks. On a ledge inside the cave he had placed a marker for each day. There were now five neat piles of seven little stones. The Sabbath's were marked with five larger rocks.

The buzz of insects out in the blazing sun lulled Jesus asleep again until he caught the scent of bread. It wafted toward him on a cool evening. breeze and floated into his mind. His lips quivered at the prospect of the fresh-baked temptation. He had dreamed of food before, but this time it seemed the bread was real.

"It's fresh-baked," the voice said. Jesus opened his eyes just in time to see his smiling visitor break the bread in half and promptly eat both pieces, chewing thoroughly and with great delight. He gave Jesus a syrupy smile. "Mmm. Delicious!" he mocked. "Why don't you give up this madness and go home? You're not the Son of God! Go home, eat, drink, enjoy life!"

Jesus looked up from his empty hands and with tired eyes answered the tempter's question with unyielding resolve. He smiled back and picked up a handful of pebbles which he let trickle from his fingers. The tempter leaned close to Jesus' ear: "If you are the Son of God, command these stones to turn into bread."

"Not on bread alone is man to live," Jesus replied, "but on every utterance that comes from the mouth of God."

✣

Today's Gospel mirrors our own temptations in life. It is so easy to yield. The right road is usually the hardest one to travel. To reach the mountain top you have to climb. The easy paths lead downhill. Jesus path ultimately led up a hill to a place called Golgotha where he paid the ultimate price. But from that cruel hilltop Jesus showed us the way to eternal life.

Second Sunday of Lent
Matthew 17: 1-9

As dazzling
as the sun!

The night wind flowed swiftly over the summit of the mountain making Jesus' hair dance about his face. The three disciples who had made the exhausting climb with him were still wheezing and wondering why he had led them through the darkness to this solitary place. Jesus held up his hand, bidding them to stay where they were. He walked away from them and stood alone beneath the star-filled sky.

The disciples watched fearfully as the wind grew stronger, beginning to moan.

Jesus waited, head bowed, and then slowly, as if he was hearing something in the rush of wind, he began to lift his face upward. As he did, Jesus began to glow. The light seemed to come from within and it grew in intensity.

Peter, James and John stood, motionless, unable to breathe, their eyes wide with astonishment and fear. Jesus was incandescent, no longer touching the ground, gazing confidently up at the light of Moses and Elijah.

Peter, overwhelmed with the vision, began to call out to Jesus but his words were swallowed by the wind and lost in the bright cloud that had suddenly formed above them.

In the roar of wind there came a powerful voice. The words tumbled down, as loud as thunder. "This is my beloved Son on whom my favor rests. Listen to him.!"

The celestial cloud, the dazzling light, the overpowering voice and the radiance of Jesus was beyond the disciples' ability to behold. Their knees collapsed and they fell to the ground, sobbing.

When Peter felt Jesus' hand gently press on his shoulder he realized he had fallen asleep. He bravely opened his eyes to the darkness. There was no more wind, no more light, just Jesus' consoling presence there in the dark.

"Get up." Jesus said, "Do not be afraid,"

Peter got to his feet and roused James and John. Following Jesus, they

started to find their way back down the dark mountain. No-one spoke. Their minds were full, trying to acknowledge what their eyes had seen and their ears had heard.

☧

The Transfiguration reveals Jesus as the fulfillment of the law and the prophets. As he did to Moses, God appears again on the mountain top. He repeats again the words he spoke at Jesus' baptism, declaring him to be his beloved Son and directing that we listen to him.

As we move through the Lenten season we are reminded that we must listen to Jesus as he works within our lives to transfigure us and bathe us in his light.

3rd Sunday in Lent
John 4: 5-42

Living water...

Jesus and his disciples were deep in Samaritan territory, about halfway between Jerusalem and Galilee. Yesterday they had walked hard all day. Now it was about noon. The sun seemed closer and hotter at these higher elevations along the slope trail near Mount Gerizim. Jesus was tired, thirsty and hungry and Jacob's Well was a welcome sight. The disciples volunteered to take a detour into the town of Shechem to buy some food while Jesus stayed near the well. He moved away from the road and finding a good spot, he sat down on the ground. Jesus' tired feet tingled as he waited for the disciples to return and looked out on the brown hills they had just traversed. The hills flattened into a broad field where so much history had taken place. This plain was a Samaritan place of worship. On these lands the Israelites had first set up an altar upon which the patriarchs had sacrificed. This was also the field that Jacob had given to his son Joseph.

A slender Samaritan woman approached the well with her empty water jar. She began to lower the roped bucket into the well. Jesus watched and remembered how thirsty he was. His dry lips opened and he called to her: "Give me a drink."

The woman brushed her hair away from her face and looked up at the foreigner sitting nearby. She studied him for a long moment and then decided he must be a Jew. Jesus smiled at her. He got to his feet and walked over to the well, standing before her and the brimming bucket of cold water.

"You are a Jew," she announced, raising her face to look up at Jesus. She dipped her cup into the water and held it out to him. "I am a Samaritan. How can you ask me for a drink?"

Jesus gently took the cup of water from her hands and lifted it to his lips. He paused for a moment and then put his lips on the cup and drank all of the water.

Heinrich Hoffman

The Samaritan woman stared in disbelief. Handing the cup back to her, Jesus began to explain. In the moments that followed the Samaritan woman would learn that Jesus was the awaited Messiah, the one who had come to bring everyone living water—a water which would become a gushing fountain with waters leaping up to provide eternal life.

✞

Jesus' encounter with the Samaritan woman at Jacob's Well lets us hear him declare that he is the anointed one who is coming. . .the Messiah! Jesus says to her "I who speak to you am he." Through the Gospel which we read and hear this day, Jesus also addresses those words to us. "I who speak to you am he." Jesus also brings to us living water which will spring forth into our lives and provide us with the gift of eternal life.

Fourth Sunday of Lent
John 9: 1-41

'Go and wash...'

The beggar had been blind from birth. He had never seen a sunrise or marveled at a sunset. His world was one of perpetual darkness and dependency.

For all of his life he had been a burden to his family—unable to shepherd the flock or do any work. As he grew to manhood he began to sense his family's thinly veiled resentment of him. Sobs of anguish would silently well up as he realized he had been a curse upon them. When he was old enough and brave enough he left home.

He made his way into the city and now was on his own. Becoming a beggar had given him his first small measure of independence. He jingled the coins in his hand and called out to attract the attention of the approaching group of voices. The blind beggar's sharp ears heard one of the men say: "Rabbi, was it his sin or his parents' that caused him to be born blind?"

The men were now standing directly in front of him and the beggar pocketed his few coins and cupped both hands together, holding them up in supplication. "Alms?" he begged, using his most hopeful tone of voice. Jesus looked down into the unseeing eyes of the beggar and felt all his sorrow.

"This man was born blind to let the works of God show forth in him," Jesus said, reaching out to touch his face. The disciples watched in silence as Jesus stooped down to crouch next to the beggar. He scooped up some dirt and spit on it to make mud. With his fingertips Jesus carefully smeared the mud on the man's eyelids. The beggar sensed something wondrous was taking place and he began to tremble, his breath coming in expectant gasps.

Jesus stood away from him and ordered "Go and wash in the Pool of Siloam the one who has been sent,"
The beggar uncupped his empty hands and carefully touched his eyelids.

He felt the mud.

The gathering crowd escorted the blind man to the pool and watched him kneel at the edge. Dipping his hands into the cool water the blind man bowed forward to wash. He scrubbed at the mud and plunged his face in the water to rinse. The coolness was always refreshing and he let his face float like a boat bottom in the dark water.

Suddenly a bright green light exploded in his head. The shock of it made him splash out to protect himself. The green light swirled into a rainbow and then rained down in crystals of color.

Philip Poteau

Gasping and sputtering he lifted his joy-filled face from the water and clutching at the robes of the man at his side, the beggar opened his eyes to behold the smiling face of Jesus.

✚

Jesus Christ, God on earth, finds a blind beggar and changes him in an instant. Jesus takes the man from despair to exquisite joy. He gives the man the gift of sight, the gift of light. The blind man did let God's works show through him. He teaches us that Jesus brings us a gift of light too. It is the light of understanding; that Jesus is the light of the world. Many are blind to this truth. To be able to truly see this we must receive his anointing and go wash the mud of sin away from our eyes. Having done this, we can open our new eyes of understanding and behold the smiling face of Jesus.

John 11: 1-45
Fifth Sunday of Lent

'Lazarus, come out!'

Lazarus of Bethany, brother of Martha and Mary, a very close friend of Jesus, lay dead, sealed inside a small cave. His body was tightly wrapped in cloth. Inside the narrow tomb it was cold, silent and black.

Suddenly Lazarus opened his eyes and the ceiling of the cave was sprayed with light. He heard the sounds of the men's voices as they moved the heavy boulder away from the mouth of the tomb. Hot, dry wind rushed into the cave and Lazarus filled his lungs with the delicious air. With the air came more light forming shadows and textures on the side walls of the cave.

Jesus' voice engulfed Lazarus. The thrilling sound swept over and around him like foaming ocean surf. His friend's words poured into Lazarus with majestic cadence and clarity. Each syllable seemed to take a century to hear but it burst upon him in only an instant. Just to hear again was exquisite. But these were words from Jesus. These were words of marvelous invitation... *"Lazarus, come out!"*

With tingling energy coursing through his veins, Lazarus responded, rolling onto his hands and knees. He crawled toward the brilliance of the day awaiting him outside the cave. At the entrance Lazarus stood erect, blinking in the bright sunlight.

Jesus waited, arms outstretched, ready to embrace him. Lazarus staggered a step closer and saw the fresh, wet tears welling up in Jesus' eyes.

"Untie him and let him go free," Jesus directed. Martha and Mary moved quickly to their re-born brother and stripped the wrappings from him. Lazarus caressed the heads of his busy sisters as they pulled the wrappings away.

The crowd which had gathered stood frozen in place. Like silent statues they watched with mouths agape. They were the true witnesses of

Plockhorst

the last and the greatest of Jesus' miracles. Even so, they could not believe what they were seeing. Their minds were already trying to find some way of explaining it.

Jesus and Lazarus embraced. What words they might have spoken would have never made it past their brimming emotions, barely contained within the fragile wall of their silence.

☦

During this Fifth Week of Lent, we listen above the roar of the world, and hear Jesus call us by name. He, invites us to 'come out' of our routines and be with him. But, like Lazarus, we are wrapped in what binds us, entombed in the world around us and powerless to rise up. But then Jesus' voice sounds within us, it awakens the power we need to rise. With Jesus' grace coursing through us, we can step into the sunlight and bask in his presence. We too shall rise.

Passion Sunday
Matthew 21: 1-11

Triumph and tragedy...

They led the donkey to him. Her back was draped with heavy cloths to make a soft saddle. Jesus hiked his robe up and swung his right leg over the animal's back and seated himself. Taking up the reins he began to ride toward mighty Jerusalem. The city's walls and parapets soared skyward just across the Kidron Valley. A large crowd cheered as Jesus approached. The disciples marched proudly behind him.

The people began making a green highway for him with hundreds of palm branches which they laid in his path.

From the topmost towers on the city wall adjoining the fortress Antonia, one of the Roman guards looked down on this moment of great triumph.

"Hey, take a look at this," he called, motioning for his fellow guard to join him at the wall.

"Who's this guy?" the other guard asked as he looked down at Jesus and his entourage making their way up the Kidron grade.

"I don't know. He might be important. You think we better report this to Quintus?"

Another intoxicating roar of greeting erupted from the crowd and James grinned happily at John. They raised their own hands sending out their "royal" greeting to the citizenry. Ahead Jesus rocked from the jerky gait of the small donkey. He was the poetic fulfillment of the Prophet Zechariah's words: "Shout for joy, Jerusalem, your king shall come to you, a just savior, meek and riding on an ass."

Jesus noticed he was gripping the reins too tightly. His forlorn expression reflected the anxiety gnawing in his heart. There he wrestled with fear of the opposite side of the moment. His triumphal ride was taking

Plockhorst

him closer his own death. In the midst of this adulation and popularity, Jesus sensed that a dark end awaited him within the walls of the city. The cheering would change to jeering.

The little donkey knew the way and kept plodding up the hill. As they passed by hundreds of welcomers lining the roadway, Jesus tried to smile. He only managed a weak grin that looked more like a grimace.

The afternoon sun beamed down on the happy faces and this moment of worldly exaltation. Too soon another afternoon sun would become dark and the thunderous sky would spark with lightning. Each crackle of blue light would paint flash images of sorrowful faces at the foot of the cross. Jesus' triumph would become tragedy and the tragedy would become his triumph.

✞

Jesus showed great courage and obedience when he entered Jerusalem for the last time. His triumphal procession on Passion Sunday is a reminder for us that all worldly triumphs are short-lived. Real triumph is born slowly from patient endurance and unswerving faith. The real kingdom is not of this world.

Easter,
John 20: 1-9.

He is risen!

Mary Magdalen lay staring up into the darkness. She was exhausted from the long hours of trying to get to sleep. There was no place she could hide from the bloody images of Jesus that had haunted her since Friday. All Sabbath night and yesterday the horror of Jesus' death had crashed against her mind like angry surf pounding against the shore. In the swirling eddies of her thoughts there would sometimes be a momentary stillness. She could relax, thinking it was all just a bad dream. But then, like a new wave being born, the reality would rise. Unable to escape, she would shudder with tearless sobs as the vicious truth reappeared and engulfed her.

Mary arose from her bed and moved soundlessly across the room. She carefully pushed the door open and peered out into the night. Her eyes searched the eastern skies for signs of morning. There was a faint, silvery tracing of light along the murky crest of the Mount of Olives. She sighed in relief. The new day was dawning at last. Now she could hurry off to meet the other women and complete the preparation of Jesus' body. Because of the Sabbath the women could not fully anoint Jesus for burial. Now that it was the first day of the week and the sabbath restriction was passed, they would be able to do their work.

She rushed through the silent streets to the garden. Mary wanted to be there ahead of the others so that she could have Jesus to herself this one last time. She would sit near the large stone that had been rolled up against the entrance to the tomb on Sabbath night. Waiting there, she knew she would find peace in his presence.

Mary Magdalen gasped at the sight of the huge stone which had been rolled away from the tomb. The others must have already arrived, and yet it was still dark. The tomb was empty. A bolt of fear coursed through her and she ran to Peter's house to tell him that Jesus was taken from the tomb. She was filled with great excitement. Her intuition already full with the knowledge that something wonderful was about to be revealed to her.

✟

The stunning realization that Jesus was risen from the dead would soon fill Mary Magdalen with a joy and peace beyond all understanding. He who had once driven the demons from her heart would now fill her heart with a love beyond all understanding. From this moment the world would be offered that same peace and love which, beyond all understanding, comes to us again in the bright hope and glory we call Easter.

Second Sunday of Easter
John 20: 19-31

'Put your hand into my side...'

Thomas hurried down the pathway between the shopkeepers stalls. The canopies overhead trapped the rich aromas of perfumes, foods and leathers which filled the air. The lengthening shadows of evening reminded Thomas that he was late for the meeting. He turned at the basketmakers and entered a dark alleyway that led to the stairs. At the top he pounded on the locked wooden door. Andrew opened it and stepped aside to let Thomas in.

The room was still hot from the heat of the day and the presence of eleven men plus the oil lamps added to the stuffiness. Thomas was uncomfortable and began to perspire from his brisk walk, the temperature and a rising anxiety about the so-called appearance of Jesus in this very place a week before. Throughout the week the others had tried unsuccessfully to convince Thomas that they had seen Jesus. The other disciples were talking nervously because there was high hope that Jesus would appear in their midst again. Thomas had seen Jesus' miracles and realized that what they said might be true. But his reason told him otherwise. Jesus was crucified and that was the end of it.

Later, when the conversations had subsided, there was a momentary lull of silence and then a sound like wings, or rain or wind. The room was suddenly cool and fresh with the clean smell of rain-drenched air. A tranquillity held every heart as Jesus was suddenly there before them. The disciples faces, reflecting Jesus' light, gasped in amazement and wonder .

"Peace be with you." Jesus said, his voice slow and soothing. Looking directly into Thomas' wide open eyes, Jesus said: "Thomas, take your finger and examine my hands. Put your hand into my side..."

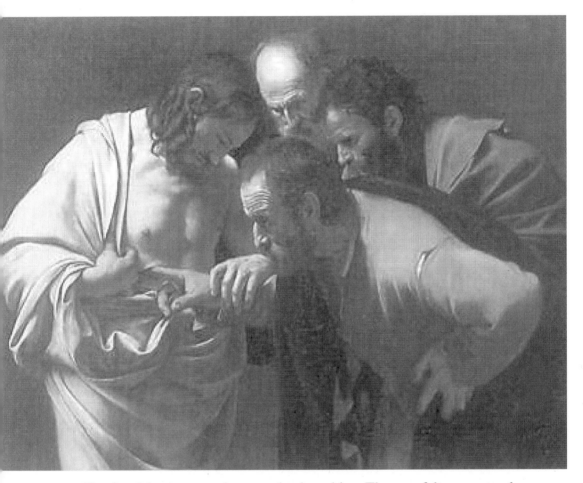

Hearing his own words come back to him, Thomas felt a great sob begin to form in the depth of his being. Hot tears were already brimming from his eyes as he extended his hand to touch the wounds in Jesus' hands and in his side. Overcome with shame, overwhelmed with grief, Thomas could barely speak his apology. His voice was a profound whisper: "My Lord and my God!"

✟

We each face a daily challenge to walk by faith and not by sight. Jesus says: "Blest are they who have not seen and have believed." John records these signs "to help you believe that Jesus is the Messiah, the Son of God, so that through this faith you may have life in his name." Easter calls us anew each year to reexamine our own faith and to be among those blessed who have not seen, but have believed.

Third Sunday of Easter,
Luke 24: 13-35

'What are you discussing?'

Walking north on the Jaffa Road, heading toward the coastal plain of Sharon, Cleopas said to his friend, "We should easily be able to reach the village of Emmaus before dark." It was only seven miles.

Cleopas continued: "We can share a nice evening meal, spend the night and continue early the next morning." His traveling companion said nothing and sighed at the prospect of all this travel.

It had been hectic getting away from Jerusalem. As always, the first day after Sabbath was doubly busy. They had stayed longer than planned, talking to Peter and the others about the shocking events concerning Jesus these last few days.

But now, at last, they were on their way. Now there was time to really talk about the crucifixion and how early this morning the women had seen a vision of angels at Jesus' empty tomb. As Cleopas chattered on, they began to walk at a fast pace, matching the excitement in his words.

Another of the people heading north along the Jaffa Road, a lone man, fell into this fast pace with Cleopas and his friend.

"What are you discussing as you go your way?" he asked them Cleopas was amazed that this man hadn't heard about the crucifixion of Jesus and told the story again. After hearing this the stranger challenged their beliefs, reminding them that all of these things had been foretold by the prophets. "Did not the Messiah have to undergo all of this to enter into his glory?" he asked them.

When they reached Emmaus the stranger was going to continue farther, but Cleopas was intrigued by his wisdom and invited him to stay with them and share a meal.

They sat together and Cleopas opened his bag and produced a loaf of bread. He handed it to the stranger who then took the loaf, broke it and then blessed the bread.

Suddenly, Cleopas and his friend recognized that it was Jesus with them. Jesus slowly and ceremoniously handed them the bread. As their eyes of understanding were opened, they all began to smile at each other.

Silently a sense of peace and love enclosed them in the moment.

Moved deeply, Cleopas bowed his head and closed his eyes. When he looked up Jesus was gone. Frozen in amazement, Cleopas could not move from where he sat. Slowly he turned his head toward his friend who was staring, wide-eyed, at where Jesus had been. Without hesitation they both rose and began to run back toward Jerusalem where they would find Peter and tell him about the miracle they had just experienced.

✟

In each of our life's journeys be assured, we will encounter Jesus along the way. He comes to us in different ways and we may not always be able to recognize him. He may come as a stranger on the road or a newcomer in our midst. He may come as an act of love from someone we know. We may see him in a time of great trial or he may simply be there smiling to us through the face of a flower, or in the sound of a song or by the glow of a sunset. May we be ever-vigilant for his presence. He is risen, He is among us here and now!

Fourth Sunday of Easter
John 10: 1-10

The Good Shepherd

Jesus lifted the latch to the gate of the sheep-fold. The disciples and some others watched in silence as he stepped into to the pen. Closing the gate behind him, Jesus began to walk through the noisy yard among the bleating sheep. The animals milled and mixed about in the tight enclosure. Jesus seemed amused as he looked them over. They were sheep from many flocks; they belonged to different local shepherds. To protect the animals it was the custom to keep the sheep in a common fold each night.

The sea of woolly gray backs parted as Jesus walked among them. Turning back to face the disciples, Jesus pointed toward the sheep-gate and said: "Whoever does not enter the sheep-fold through the gate, but climbs in some other way, is a thief and a marauder."

Placing his hands flat against his chest, Jesus declared: "The one who enters through the gate is shepherd of the sheep…he walks in front of them and the sheep follow him because they recognize his voice."

As he spoke Jesus opened the big gate again and led the flock out toward the green pasture. Only his own sheep followed him. The others stayed in the fold. They would not follow any other shepherd. They would wait for their own to come for them.

The group of men, most of them Jesus' disciples, looked on pleasantly as Jesus led the sheep. Some of them still did not get the message Jesus was trying to teach. They weren't picturing themselves as the sheep and Jesus as their true shepherd…the one who speaks with God's voice.

Jesus seemed to know they needed more, so he made it clearer: "I am the sheep-gate…whoever enters through me will be safe. He will go in and out and find pasture."

The men began to nod, smile and speak among themselves as Jesus' ideas began to arrange themselves in their minds.

Plockhorst

✝

Is Jesus your good shepherd? Do you recognize his voice in your life? Do you follow his lead? Do you believe the Good Shepherd Jesus knows you by name?

Jesus says that he is not only the shepherd, but that he is the gate as well. In this teaching we come to understand that it is only through this gate, through him, that we can enjoy life everlasting. As he said himself: "I came that you might have life and have it to the full."

Fifth Sunday of Easter
John 14: 1-10

'Do not let your hearts be troubled'

The disciples were slowly coming to understand that this was the last supper they would share with Jesus. It was hard to believe because only a few days ago when they had all entered Jerusalem Jesus was hailed as a king. Some of the disciples had been imagining great things for themselves in Jesus' new earthly kingdom.

But now it was vanishing like a dream in the morning light. Jesus had just told them he was going to leave them. He said they could not follow. All of their expectations were collapsing around them like a house of cards.

Jesus folded his hands in his lap and looked around the room at the sad faces of his closest followers. Some looked away with worried faces. Others had a look of astonishment on their faces. Peter was doubly shocked because he was still wrestling with Jesus having told him he would deny him three times before that night would end. They were devastated.

Jesus heart swelled with compassion and he told them: "Do not let your hearts be troubled. Have faith in God and faith in me." He told them he was going to prepare a place for them and that he would come back for them. Jesus said: "You know the way that leads where I go."

Thomas was quick to question this. He could contain himself no longer and declared he did not know the way. Jesus smiled his reassurance at poor Thomas, knowing that he always needed proof. Then his face became solemn as Jesus declared: "I am the way, and the truth, and the life; no one comes to the Father but through me. If you really knew me, you would know my Father also."

✝

In our lives there are times when we may feel like the disciples, worried that Jesus has abandoned us. Even Jesus asked the Father "why have you abandoned me?" But the Good News and the truth is that he has not abandoned us and never will. Jesus has gone to prepare a place for us so that where he is we may also be. That is why Jesus says to each of us: "Do not let your hearts be troubled."

Sixth Sunday of Easter
John 14:15-21

A helper, to be with you always

Peter's face was reddened with the flush of wine. It darkened further as his frustrations festered. Jesus was leaving them and this was their final meal together. It was all over! Suddenly, everything was going wrong. And worse, Peter had been accused of unfaithfulness.

Peter took another swallow of his wine and pondered how he could ever deny this Jesus whom he had followed all over Galilee and Samaria for the last three years.

Unable to contain his wrath, Peter blurted out: "I don't get it! What are we supposed to do if you leave us?"

Jesus leaned over and put his hand on Peter's back. In loving, patient words, Jesus explained: "If you love me and obey the commands I give you, I will ask the Father and he will give you another helper to be with you always..."

Peter thought Jesus was announcing someone new. Another Messiah?

Jesus continued: "...the Spirit of truth, whom the world cannot accept, since it neither sees him nor recognizes him, but you can recognize him because he remains with you and will be within you."

Peter felt a rush of anger. "No! We don't want another Spirit. You're abandoning us like orphans," he charged.

Jesus gave reassurance, "I will not leave you orphaned, I will come back to you."

Thomas called out: "When? When will this happen?'"

Jesus went on: "A little while now and the world will see me no more; but you see me as one who has life, and you will have life. On that day you will know that I am in my Father, and you in me, and I in you."

These words of Jesus were faint signs of hope for them, bursting like distant fireworks in the night. In the flash of light they perceived the bright, clear ideas. But fear and doubt quickly dissolved the insights, leaving the disciples awash in darkness again.

Understanding this, Jesus gave the disciples further reassurance He

explained that if they loved him, the Father would love them back, and that he would love them and reveal himself to them.

It was too much. The disciples yearned for yesterday's peace, but the wail of tomorrow had already begun. A pall of anxiety cloaked their certainty that something terrible was about to happen.

☩

Jesus' words to the disciples at the last supper gave the assurance that the Spirit would come and be with them always. Jesus said that we would see what the world does not see.

In the Liturgy of the Eucharist Jesus' promise is fulfilled. It is in the breaking of the bread that we remember what he said: "You will see me" because "on that day you will know that I am in my Father, and you in me, and I in you."

Ascension
Matthew 28: 16-20

'...until the end
of the world'

John, one of the younger disciples, was well ahead of the other ten who were slowly making their way up the steep mountainside. Jesus had summoned them and they were hurrying to the top of the mountain where they hoped he would be waiting for them.

The slowest of the disciples was Peter, clutching his robe to his chest as he struggled to keep up. His eyes bulged from his red face as he gasped for more air. Unable to continue without rest, Peter stopped to survey the grassy slopes which flowed down to the blue waters of the Sea of Galilee. Turning back, to look up ahead, Peter watched his brother Andrew, climbing steadily with Simon and Thomas.

Farther up the trail James and his son, Thaddeus, were walking with Philip. Beyond them Bartholomew, young James and Matthew were talking about each of the appearances of Jesus since the Crucifixion. They had seen him in the upper room, Mary had encountered him in the garden, he had been seen on the road to Emmaus and also on the shore of the lake at breakfast time. It was all too much to believe! Still, there was no denying it. They had seen him with their own eyes. It was terrifying to realize.

When John was close to the summit he saw Jesus coming forward to meet him. As the others arrived the sight of Jesus filled them with emotion and they dropped to their knees. Tears brimmed in their eyes and each of the disciples fell forward in complete submission to the God who stood before them.

The voice of the Risen Christ began to speak to them. At Jesus' words they struggled to their feet. Like soft thunder, his voice reached inside them. Full of authority, he gave clear directives to make all nations his disciples...to baptize and teach them.

Jesus' commands were sealed with a final profession of his love for them. He said "And know that I am with you always until the end of the world."

And then he was gone.

Plockhorst

✠

　　These love-filled words of Jesus before his ascension, are the last recorded. As soon as he spoke them, Jesus rose on a cloud which took him from sight. The disciples stood together on the mountain summit staring up at the now empty sky. A wind began to flow over them as the silence drowned the beat of their pounding hearts. Today we are on that mountain top with them and the words which Jesus spoke to them now become words spoken to us. We are called to carry on his work and also to know that he is also with each of us unto the end of our world.

Pentecost
John 20: 19-23

'Receive the Holy Spirit'

The ten disciples had just seen Jesus disappear. Crowded together in the upper room they sat in silence, staring at the emptiness where he had just been.

Earlier Jesus had suddenly appeared before them, coming in a dazzling light. He had spoken wonderful words. Then, just as he had come, he suddenly dissolved, taking his light with him.

In the dusky light of the room the flames from the oil lamps flickered, splashing an eerie yellow upon the circle of disciples. No-one could speak. They were still in rapture from his presence.

Recalling what Jesus had said to them, Peter's lips began to move silently as he repeated the words of Jesus. Then he broke the silence: '...as the Father has sent me, so I send you." The others looked over at Peter, honoring his leadership and waiting for further explanation.

"Each of us must teach others what Jesus has taught us," Peter said. "He has breathed his life into us! He has filled us with his promised holy spirit. Now we must begin to do his will."

Thaddeus spoke up: "What did our Lord mean about sins and about us forgiving them?"

Peter answered: "He said 'Receive the Holy Spirit. If you forgive sins, they are forgiven. If you don't forgive them, they are not forgiven."

They all fell into a silence, repeating Jesus' words to themselves. As they spoke the words in their minds, Jesus' power claimed them. They had just inherited the Church. Infused with the Spirit, they were eager to begin.

Peter cleared his throat and they all looked at him. He opened his hands, as if releasing a bird to fly to them. His gesture was a challenge for them to begin the work that Jesus had left for them.

Ready to begin, but not knowing in which direction, young Thaddeus stood up to ask: "What do we do now?"

And then everybody began to speak at once.

✝

As Jesus filled the disciples with his Holy Spirit that Sunday night, he will come also to us, providing we have made room for him in our lives.

Like the disciples going to the upper room, we must go to a place where Jesus can appear to us. Such a place might be at our church, but it could just as well be the silence of our heart. Wherever it is, there we must wait in joyful hope for his coming.

As we wait, we must clear our minds to receive the Holy Spirit. Hearts that are full of other wants and desires are like busy schedules with no time left to receive visitors. We must make room in our hearts for the Holy Spirit.

Once filled with the Spirit, we, like Thaddeus, may be asking the life-changing question: "What do we do now?"

Most Holy Trinity
John 3: 16-18

'For God so loved the world...'

The moonlight brightened his white robe as Nicodemus hurried to meet Jesus. Nicodemus' face was in shadow, but his eyes burned with faith in the amazing works of Jesus, the man he had secretly begun to follow.

Jesus was waiting for him at the bench near the olive tree. They greeted each other and then sat down together. Jesus waited for the first question.

As a prominent Jewish leader, Nicodemus was risking his high position. Jesus was opposed by the local officials so Nicodemus came by night to avoid being seen with this "dangerous magician." Nicodemus was a Pharisee, a strict Jewish sect that observed all of the Mosaic Laws. More importantly, Nicodemus was also one of the elite 72-members of the Sanhedrin, the highest governing council in all of Judaism. Despite his high office, Nicodemus came to visit Jesus. He had seen the miracles and had openly declared that Jesus was a "teacher come from God." Then Jesus told him "No-one can see the kingdom of God unless he is born again."

Nicodemus asked "How can a grown man be born again? How can this be?"

Jesus gently prodded Nicodemus, "You are a great teacher in Israel and still you do not know this?"

Nicodemus bent close, listening harder as Jesus explained, a person is "...born spiritually of the Spirit." He finished, saying, "...the Son of Man must be lifted up, that all who believe may have eternal life in him."

Somewhere, outside, the chirps of a night bird sounded above them. Nicodemus barely noticed it as he thought deeply about this promise of eternal life.

Once again, Nicodemus asked. "Why?"

Jesus answered: "God so loved the world that he gave his only Son, that whoever believes in him may not die but may have eternal life."

Nicodemus put his fingers to his forehead trying to massage understanding into his mind.

Jesus went on, "God did not send his Son into the world to be its judge, but to be its savior."

The moon slid behind a cloud and the garden darkened. Nicodemus sat for a long time, considering the words which Jesus had spoken. He would remember them again on that dark future day when he would purchase large quantities of costly myrrh and aloes to take to Jesus' tomb. There, Nicodemus and Joseph of Arimathea would wrap the lifeless body in a white shroud and lay him to rest. On that day Nicodemus would fully understand the depth of God's love for the world.

Trinity Sunday reminds us how much God the Father loves us: by sending his only Son to be our savior and letting us be born again in the Spirit. Those who have experienced the monumental grief of losing a son or daughter can better know the depth of God's love in giving up his only Son to die on a cross. This Father God sends his Son and the Spirit to power and sustain our lives.

Body and Blood of Christ
John 6: 51-58

'The one who eats this bread will live forever.'

The synagogue at Capernaum was filled to capacity. Inside, Jesus was teaching and the local leaders of the Jewish faith were challenging his bold statements. The people who listened were amazed at the young miracle-worker who faced off against the old rabbis.

Jesus had made Capernaum his headquarters after being rejected at Nazareth. He had come down from the hills to begin ministry in this worldly city of 10,000 people. Located on the northwest shores of the Sea of Galilee, the town was a busy fishing center. Capernaum was also a major stop on the routes to the east and did a brisk business from the caravans. With money to be collected, Capernaum had its share of tax collectors, among them Paul. Overseeing it all was the Roman garrison there.

From his seat Jesus let his voice fill the Synagogue. "I am the living bread that came down from heaven."

Such bold words brought gasps from the old men and rabbis who were there. Even though Jesus had performed miracles for them, these skeptics scoffed at this outrageous assertion. Those who knew Jesus from Nazareth asked aloud: "Isn't he the carpenter's son. We know his parents. How can he claim to come down from heaven?"

Jesus continued despite their scorn. "If anyone eats this bread he will live forever. The bread that I will give is my flesh, which I give so that the world may live."

At this the room became a babble of angry voices. One rabbi got to his feet and began to move toward Jesus.

Jesus stood himself and extending his hands above the assembly he shouted into the furor: "Whoever eats my flesh and drinks my blood has eternal life and I will raise him up to life on the last day."

The old rabbi came up and sputtered his indignation at Jesus. Many followed him as he left the room, unable to accept Jesus' truth.

Jesus sat back down and folded his hands in his lap. Many of the men remained, sitting with Jesus in the silence. They looked at him in wonder, remembering his enticing words: "The one who eats this bread will live forever."

✛

The idea that Jesus was the Messiah, sent by God, was too difficult for many to grasp. Later Jesus even challenged his own disciples with the question: "And you, would you also like to leave?"

As Jesus-followers today, we have not left. We've come to hear this Sunday's Gospel and his wondrous words: "The one who feeds on my flesh and drinks my blood remains in me and I in him." This invites us to a miraculous exchange. In Eucharist Jesus dwells in us and by this Communion we remain in Christ!

11th Sunday in Ordinary Time
Mt. 9:36 to 10:8

'Go and preach!'

Simon, the zealot, looked over at Peter to check his reaction. Jesus had just commissioned his disciples, giving them the power to heal and to drive out evil spirits. Peter glanced down at his hands to see if this new power had somehow changed them.

Earlier that day, the crowds in and around the synagogue were so thick that Jesus and the disciples had to struggle to get out of the building. Once outside they were still surrounded by walls of people. Gently pushing their way, they worked toward the street, hoping to escape to Peter's boat.

They hurried down the road toward the water's edge. When they had gained a little distance Jesus paused. He turned back to face the river of people flowing after him. The crowd also stopped, hoping Jesus would speak to them again. Jesus could see many were still streaming out of the synagogue. Their faces were hopeful and their eyes were hungry.

Jesus' heart went out to them. He wanted to help each one, but there were too many. He couldn't do it alone. He needed to commission his disciples.

Turning away from the crowds, Jesus faced the Twelve, saying: "The harvest is large, but there are few workers to gather it in."

In Galilee a good harvest was a great blessing and it was unthinkable to waste any of it, so Jesus continued: "Pray to the owner of the harvest that he will send workers to gather it in."

Later that night, Jesus explained to the disciples that they were the workers who were sent to gather in this great harvest of people. He told them they would be given the power to drive out evil spirits — to heal every disease and sickness. It was then that Peter had glanced down at his hands and Simon, the zealot, had noticed.

They were both solemnly looking into each others eyes when Jesus commanded them to "Go and preach! The Kingdom of Heaven is near!"

The fat red sun was sinking behind the western mountains. Soon night would blanket them in deep thoughts. With the dawning of the new day, like the first flames of a new fire, the disciples would spread out and go forth to preach and teach.

✠

The commissioning of Jesus' disciples reveals to us that we are also commissioned. We are the workers sent to reap today's harvest.

We must preach the message that "the Kingdom of Heaven is near!' To do that we must first preach that message to ourselves. Until we have truly heard it we cannot bring the message to others. But, once we know, our faith will enable and empower us to do our part in God's great harvest.

12th Sunday in Ordinary Time
Mt. 10: 26-33

Once upon
a summer's night...

Peter's boat was anchored and tied to shore in the waist-deep inner cove at Capernaum. The lake was settling down for the night, leaving only a gentle surge to slowly rock the old boat. Jesus was sitting near the bow facing back toward his disciples. He was barely visible in the dark— only his pale robe showed against the darker sky.

At sunset they had all waded out to the boat to escape the crowds. Since then, Jesus had been teaching his disciples with such intensity that no one noticed that the night had closed in around them. The moon was soon to rise, but now, in the blackness, there was only Jesus' voice, soft, like a warm blanket about them.

"What I am telling you in the dark," he said to them, "you must repeat in broad daylight,".

One of the disciples questioned, "Aren't these things you've told us to be secrets for us alone to know?"

Jesus shook his head, hoping to prepare his disciples for their own future ministry when they would be on their own. "What you have heard in private, you must announce from the housetops." It was a warning not to be afraid, even of death. The greater danger would be to lose their souls.

A silence fell over the men as they pondered what Jesus was saying. It was late and they had been sitting in the boat for a long time. Jesus knew they were tired and so was he. The moon was rising with light to lead them home.

One by one they climbed over the gunwale of the boat and dropped into the chilling water to wade ashore. The last one off was Peter who had stayed to make sure the lines were secured.

Jesus waited for him and together they walked toward Peter's house where Jesus was staying. Peter began to grumble about losing his soul.

Jesus assured him that the Father loved him more than he knew. "Are not two sparrows sold for next to nothing? Yet not a single sparrow falls to the ground without your Father's consent." Jesus gave Peter's shaggy hair a friendly tug. "As for you, every hair of your head has been counted; so do not be afraid of anything. You are worth far more than even an entire flock of sparrows."

The moon was climbing behind them and they could see their faint shadows stretching ahead. Jesus put his hand on Peter's shoulder, pulling him to a stop. They faced each other in the silver light as Jesus made his final point.

"Peter, whoever acknowledges me before others, I will acknowledge before my Father in heaven. Whoever disowns me before others I will disown before my Father in heaven."

Peter smiled back confidently. He knew he would always follow his great friend, Jesus. He knew he would always acknowledge Jesus before the world. If ever anything was certain, Peter knew he would never disown Jesus.

✞

Today's Gospel demands that we think about the strength of our own faith. We need to consider more than just our Sunday best. We must also face our Wednesday worst! Will we always follow our great friend, Jesus? Will we always acknowledge Jesus before others or by our silence will we disown Jesus?

13th Sunday in Ordinary Time
Mt. 10: 37-42

'Whoever loses their life for my sake, will gain it.'

Jesus had heard enough of the disciples' stupid talk! He finished his wine with two large swallows and tossed his cup aside. Then, he abruptly got up to leave.

"Teacher, where are you going" one of them called after him. But Jesus was too frustrated to answer. He stalked up the hillside until the disciples were far enough away for their voices to be muffled by the wind. Jesus looked down on them, reclining on the grass, still gabbing and gesturing as they finished their meal.

A wave of hopelessness swamped Jesus. His disciples still didn't seem to have the faintest notion of what he had been trying to teach them all these months. They were still selfishly thinking about what they could get for themselves. They enjoyed the respect people showed them because they were members of Jesus' party. Some expected "the kingdom" was going to bring worldly power and wealth to them. They seemed to just be following Jesus for the money.

Jesus bowed his head and prayed. After a moment, a new energy and deep peace began to flow into him. He realized that his frustration with his disciples was partly his own fear of the future when he must take up his cross and lose his own life for them. Jesus' thoughts turned to face down the lurking death-beast that haunted him. He did not want to leave these sweet hills of home—these love-filled faces of his friends.

Quickly, he opened his eyes and saw that the disciples had all risen to their feet and were gazing back at him. Jesus waded through the grass, hurrying back to them. He was ready to resume the difficult teaching.

Young Thaddeus was standing by his father, James. Jesus looked directly at Thaddeus, "Whoever loves his father or mother more than me is not fit to be my disciple;" then turning his eyes to James, Jesus went on: "whoever loves his son or daughter more than me is not fit to be my disciple."

Then, taking them all in his gaze, he said "Whoever does not take up his cross and follow in my steps is not fit to be my disciple." Jesus knew these were harsh words. but they were necessary for what he was going to say next.

"Whoever tries to gain his own life will lose it; but whoever loses his life for my sake will gain it." The disciples fell silent, trying to understand.

John was the first to smile. Suddenly the proposition made sense to him and he began to nod his head in agreement.

"Amen, teacher, Amen!" he said.

✟

Giving up our life for Jesus means more than just "to die." We must be willing to give up our worldly things, like money. It means we must give up bad habits that can destroy us.. It means we have to give up time doing things we like in order to spend time with Jesus. But, like balancing the scales, it is in giving that we receive. When we give we usually get something in return. With Jesus the gift is new life. As Christians we not only enjoy a new life here in the present world, we also receive the promise of new life in the world to come.

Fourteenth Sunday in Ordinary Time
Mt. 11: 25-30

'My yoke is easy and my burden is light.'

The River Jordan flowed due south, almost as straight as a Roman aqueduct. It was a watery thread that ran for nearly 70 miles to the brackish waters of Lake Asphaltus, choking in salt at the bottom of the deepest valley in the world. The banks of the Jordan made a reasonably level road for merchants and travelers heading down from Galilee towards Jerusalem.

Jesus and his friends were beginning the last day's journey up to Bethany toward Jerusalem. From Jericho they began the hard climb up to the great walled city, perched in the highlands 2,500 feet above the hot river valley.

They climbed steadily and silently with the warm morning sun slowly baking their backs. The uphill grade was really taking its toll on Peter whose red face was glistening with sweat. He trudged up the trail with his heavy bag of belongings slung from his shoulder.

Jesus was silent, wrestling with his own deep thoughts about the Father. It was frightening for him to carry the awesome reality that he and the Father were one inside this fragile human body. Jesus shook his head. It was too much to bear.

Yet, his relationship with God was absolutely certain. It could not be denied any more than he could deny the power he possessed. He was the Son of God! This mystery, even to Jesus, was beginning to be understood by his friends and followers. Sometimes these simple men seemed to comprehend this vast idea. Jesus thought it ironic that the intellectuals and rabbis, with all their knowledge of God's laws, could never allow themselves to believe the truth that Jesus claimed before them.

Peter was starting to wheeze and groan so Jesus stepped off the road to give everyone a short rest. Peter grimaced as he lowered himself to sit on his bag. The others gathered around them, easing their bags to the ground. It looked to them like Jesus was going to make an announcement so they waited in silence.

Jesus squinted in the bright sunlight and looked beyond his disciples. He seemed to be searching for something in the sky. Then he began to pray, "Father, I thank you because you have shown to the unlearned what you have hidden from the wise." Jesus' dry lips widened to a smile as he looked over his little group of simple men. He felt proud of them. They were in the process of learning the great mystery. They were richly blessed because through Jesus they would know God better than anyone before or since.

"Come to me, all of you who are tired of carrying heavy loads, and I will give you rest." Jesus said. Take my yoke and put it on you, and learn from me, because I am gentle and humble in spirit; and you will find rest. For the yoke I will give you is easy and the load I put upon you is light."

Jesus then moved out, climbing steadily up the Bethany road. Peter sighed and lifted his heavy sack and began slogging uphill after Jesus. Suddenly Peter's bag grew light. He looked to see if all the contents had somehow spilled out. Everything was still inside the bulging pack, yet it felt light.

Peter looked up at Jesus, questioning how this could be. The Master glanced back at Peter and gave him a knowing smile. "My yoke is easy and my burden is light," Jesus repeated.

✝

We modern-day disciples are challenged to understand that Jesus was both man and God. Modern day disciples are challenged to pick up the yoke of faith and wear it. In doing so we can learn that Jesus' yoke does indeed make it easier to bear the burdens we already have.

Fifteenth Sunday in Ordinary Time
Matthew 13: 1-23

Seeds of Faith

The morning sun streamed through the window of Peter's house where Jesus was a guest. Peter and the others had gone off to attend to various errands and Jesus was enjoying the silence and the solitude. He studied the intense red flowers peeking up at him over the ledge of the window. The blossoms seemed to explode with color as each petal flared out to receive the full light of the sun. "What a marvel that such beauty could grow from a tiny seed!" Jesus almost said aloud.

Jesus was still considering the unleashed power contained within seeds as he decided to wander down to the lake. Perhaps Peter was there at the boat. Stepping out into the day, Jesus sensed the summer's warmth. Walking beneath the big shade trees he heard the chattering birds above him, busy in their little world. It was going to be a wonderful day!

Peter was not on the boat, so Jesus sat on one of the big flat rocks that edged the little harbor of Capernaum. He began to chat with some of the fishermen there. Word quickly spread that "the Teacher" was at the lake. Jesus was soon surrounded by so many people that he waded out to Peter's boat and climbed in. Speaking from there he began to share his thoughts:

"One day a farmer went out sowing. Part of what he sowed landed on a footpath, where birds came and ate it up. Part of it fell on rocky ground where it had little soil…and it began to wither for lack of roots. Part of the seed fell among the thorn bushes which grew up and choked it. Part of it landed on good soil and yielded grain at 100 or 60 or 30-fold."

Jesus continued to tell his parable stories from the platform of Peter's boat. Later in the morning most of the disciples joined the crowd on the shore. About noon Jesus blessed the crowd and sent them on their way.

That afternoon Peter invited the other disciples to share their mid-day meal out on the boat. Still chewing, with bread crumbs falling on his beard, James questioned Jesus: "Why do you speak to the crowds in parables?"

Jesus answered, "I use parables when I speak to them because they look , but do not see; they listen, but do not hear or understand."

They all sat in silence for a moment. Then Jesus reached out to put his hands on them and warmly praised them, "But blest are your eyes because they see and blest are your ears because they hear."

☦

The familiar parable of the sower is much more than a story about the fate of some seeds. It is about us—our past, our present and our future! As "seeds" we may have fallen on difficult ground. We may find ourselves today in need of nourishment, protection and deeper roots. The seeds of our faith need constant attention...watered with the Word, and warmed by the Son, and constantly "weeded" by our own hard work.

Sixteenth Sunday in Ordinary Time
Matthew 13: 24-43

Seeds, weeds and the yeast of faith

The people enjoyed the way Jesus talked to them. His parables made everything easy to remember. Wrapped in a story, his message was alive and continued to live in their minds.

Jesus reached down and picked up a tiny mustard seed. He carefully held it between his finger and this thumb. Closing one eye he focused on the miniature seed, holding it up at eye level and turned in a half circle so that all gathered around him could see.

"The Kingdom of Heaven is like this," Jesus announced, allowing them time to murmur among themselves. Some of the people were wondering how a little seed could be like the Kingdom of Heaven. How could you get a palace, a temple, all the people and everything else into a little seed? Jesus went on to explain that even though the mustard seed is the smallest of seeds it would one day grow into a tree. It would be a tree so large that birds would build their nests in its branches.

To further explain the Kingdom of God, he told them the parable about the woman adding yeast to the flour and then watching the dough grow. For yet another example of what the Kingdom of God is like he gave them the parable about the enemy who sowed weeds in among the wheat.

That night after Jesus returned to Peter's house, some of the disciples showed up. Jesus had been lying down and rose up on one elbow when they entered the house. He yawned as he watched them seat themselves on cushions along the front wall.

"Sorry if we woke you up," one of them said. "It's okay", Jesus smiled. Peter grinned at Jesus' unlikely statement and rolled his eyes in mock disbelief.

Felter

But Matthew was eager with a serious question. He leaned forward, addressing Jesus: "Tell us, what does the story about the weeds in the field mean?"

Jesus answered quickly: "The man who sowed the good seed is the Son of Man; the field is the world; the good seeds are the people who belong to the Kingdom; the weeds are the people who belong to the Evil One; and the enemy who sowed the seeds is the Devil. The harvest is the end of the age, and the harvest workers are the angels."

Jesus saw in their faces that the parable had become astonishingly clear to them.

The disciples were "good seeds" but "weeds" would be sewn among them. At that Judas felt a cold shadow of uneasiness pass over him. When he looked up Judas saw that Jesus was looking directly at him. Their eyes met for a moment, then Judas looked down again and pretended to be in deep thought.

☦

Jesus continues to teach us with his wonderful parables. This Sunday's Gospel invites us to think about seeds, yeast and weeds. Underlying these stories are images of hope and great growth despite great difficulties. It sounds a lot like the stuff of Life! It also sounds a lot like a promise that God's people will one day "...shine like the sun in their Father's Kingdom."

Seventeenth Sunday in Ordinary Time
Matthew 13: 44-52

Three Lessons

Jesus liked Capernaum. There was something special about being at a place where the water joined the land. The solid shore and the restless sea were like a crossroads where water, land and sky converged. It was a good place to balance the present day against the uncertain future.

On hot days Capernaum's fishing harbor was also a great place to cool off.

This day's heat had been suffocating. It was evening and still impossible to be indoors. Hundreds of townspeople, among them Jesus, had gone down to the harbor to seek the night breezes which were beginning to blow in from the lake.

Jesus stepped out of his sandals and waded into the cool water. He turned to face the crowd sitting on the grassy bank. Jesus had been preaching to them about the "kingdom."

One of them said, "How can you say these things? We can't just drop everything to follow you!"

Jesus smiled at Simon Peter and Andrew who were also sitting on the bank. Pointing toward them, he said, "They did."

An old fishermen rose to his feet, shaking his accusing finger at Jesus: "How are Simon and Andrew supposed to feed their families when they've left their boats in this harbor? They can't fish if they are going to follow you?"

Jesus said: "When you see the treasure that the Kingdom has for you, the choice to follow is casy." He continued, trying make them understand that there are greater treasures than a good catch of fish. He told them that the kingdom of God is a treasure which offers untold wealth if they would look and see it.

It was the time of the full moon and as it began to rise, full and fat, from across the lake, the moonlight became a silver edge around Jesus' figure.

Another old man asked, "What is this kingdom you are talking about? What is heaven?"

"Heaven is like this…" Jesus paused, letting their anticipation build. "A man happens to find a treasure hidden in a field. He covers it up again, and is so happy that he goes and sells everything he has, and then goes back and buys that field."

Jesus then gave them another story about the man looking for fine pearls who, when he finds one, sells everything he has to buy it.

It was still too hot to go home and the crowd seemed eager for more examples, so Jesus told them a fishing story.

"The Kingdom of Heaven is also like this," he said, "Some fishermen throw their net out in the lake and catch all kinds of fish. When the net is full, they pull it to shore and sit down to divide the fish: the good ones go into the buckets, the worthless ones are thrown away." Jesus explained it would be like this for people; the good are kept, and the evil ones are thrown away.

When they wanted to hear even more, Jesus told them that every teacher who becomes a discile in the Kingdom is like a homeowner who takes both new and old things out of his storage room.

Jesus waded back ashore letting the grass dry the bottoms of his feet. As he moved among the people he searched their faces, hoping that they had understood that they are like the homeowner. They now have both the old law of the prophets and the new law of the Gospel.

Jesus sat down on the grass in their midst. No one spoke. They just sat together on the bank gazing out at the dark lake letting the peacefulness, the breeze and the moonlight wash over them.

✠

Jesus continues to teach us with his wonderful parables as this Sunday's Gospel invites us to discover the treasure of the kingdom in our own lives. It's buried in our hearts. We need only to uncover it. When we find it we will gladly give everything we have to possess it.

18th Sunday in Ordinary Time
Matthew 14: 13-21

The twelve baskets

Peter's eyes were glazed over. He seemed to be in shock, jabbering and muttering to himself as he filled his basket with chunks of bread and pieces of fish which the crowd had been unable to eat.

"I know there only five loaves to start with!" he told himself, trying to reason it out. Yet, the ground was still covered with crumbs. Seeing the white crumbs on the ground made him remember how God had showered manna onto the desert to feed his wandering forefathers. Peter's basket was nearly full but he still had much more to pick up.

Glancing at the adjoining section of people, Peter saw his brother Andrew also harvesting bread crumbs. Then he turned and continued to gather.

Darkness was closing in and soon all twelve disciples returned to Jesus bringing their brimming baskets of what was left from the five loaves and the two fishes.

Jesus slowly looked over the twelve baskets that had been set before him. The lines of exhaustion were set deep in his face. He still mourned the news of John's death at the hands of Herod. The relentless hounding of the people had consumed what was left of his energy. He rose and touched the baskets—mute evidence of his great miracle. The disciples around him stood in silence. No-one seemed able to believe what had just happened.

Jesus' then went around and touched each of his twelve followers, laying his hand on their backs and gripping their sturdy shoulders. As he did so, Jesus was thinking of a final breaking of the bread they would share all too soon.

"I need some time," Jesus said to them. "You go ahead without me. Take the boat and leave for Capernaum. I'll be along later."

✞

Jesus continues to feed us with the Eucharist. This miracle story invites us to join the disciples in the realization that God will take care of us. At this time in our lives we may be in a "deserted place." We may think that we are far from any help. We may feel abandoned and hopeless. But Jesus is with us, the same yesterday, today and tomorrow. He is present in every moment of our life. He empowers us to take our meager resources and multiply them by our faith and by our action.

19th Sunday in Ordinary Time
Matthew 14: 22-33

Footprints on the sea

Peter's heavy fishing boat had been slamming into the whitecapped waves for six hours. In the black midnight Peter sat on the stern thwart and tried to steer a course for Capernaum. As he strained to hold the big tiller steady the howling wind flattened his beard against his weary face. Even if this night squall subsided they would probably be unable to reach Capernaum before sunrise.

Four of the disciples were rowing, each manning one of the long oars. The sail was furled, useless as they rowed against the stiff wind. Progress was painful as they inched their way toward the distant harbor.

The other seven disciples spaced themselves around the boat trying to rest before it was their turn to row again. But sleep was hopeless in the fearful noise of the gale which was getting worse.

Earlier that night Jesus told the disciples to take the boat and leave without him. When they left for Capernaum the weather was calm. Then the sudden storm had risen to full fury. Their leftover baskets of bread were drenched from the heavy spray.

Peter thought of Jesus, somewhere ashore, miles behind them, wishing he was there too. But there was no easy way out. They were struggling in the middle of the Sea of Galilee, halfway to Capernaum. Survival meant keeping the bow facing into the waves. They had to keep rowing, all night long if necessary.

Peter clung grimly to the tiller, refusing to let anyone relieve him. Three more hours dragged by. The sun would not be up for another three hours and Peter was beginning to wonder if he could last until daybreak.

Suddenly one of the disciples began to shout hysterically, "What's that, what's that, what's that?"

Peter looked astern and was terrified to see a pale light moving rapidly toward the boat. All the others were alarmed and tried to get to their feet to see what was happening. When the ghostly light drew closer they saw that it appeared to be a man—a man who was walking on the water. Exhausted from the long, sleepless night, the disciples froze in fear before the

nightmare that was taking place before their eyes. Some were unable to
face the vision and cowered in the bottom of the boat. When Peter saw that
the ghost was Jesus he lost control of the tiller. The boat rolled broadside to
the waves, dipping a rail under the black sea. Cold water sloshed over the
side, soaking the disciples and sending them all into a screaming panic.

Jesus called across the water: "Courage," he said, "It is I. Do not be
afraid."

☩

*In our darkest night, when we face something that seems
overwhelming, is there anyone who can save us? When we face our own
death is there anyone who can save us? Our faith teaches us not to be
afraid because Jesus is with us always. Our faith invites us to step with
Peter out onto the water. Our faith will hold us up as long as it is strong
enough. Today's Gospel invites us to join the disciples in the boat when
after Jesus calmed the water, they praised him, exclaiming: "Truly you are
the Son of God!"*

20th Sunday in Ordinary Time
Matthew 15: 21-28

Encounter in Phoenicia

In the Spring of his third year of ministry, Jesus and his disciples journeyed northwest into new territories. All the day before they had followed the Jordan north from the Sea of Galilee to reach Lake Huleh. The next morning they climbed the lonely hills and entered the region called Phoenicia. The peace of these empty hills restored Jesus after the constant crowds that had hounded him in Galilee.

Once they were through the highest passes, the road was easier, meandering gradually down to meet the brimming Mediterranean Sea. The bustling seaport city of Tyre was now only a day's walk away.

Once an island, Tyre jutted boldly out into the blue waters. Three centuries before, Tyre was joined to the mainland when the armies of Alexander the Great, after a seven-month seige, built a causeway to reach and conquer the island.

Jesus and the disciples took lodging at a house some distance outside Tyre. They hoped to go unnoticed. But a Canaanite woman, who had followed them, came close to the house and began to call out: "Son of David, have mercy on me!" From inside the house Jesus heard her calling, asking him to heal her daughter, who was possessed by a demon.

James urged Jesus: "Send her away." But the woman persisted, shouting all the louder for Jesus to come out and save her daughter.

Finally, Jesus went to the doorway and told the woman: "I have been sent only to the lost sheep of Israel." It didn't matter to her that she was not an Israelite. She threw herself at Jesus' feet and begged him: "Help me!" Jesus responded with a saying: "It isn't right to take the children's food and throw it to the dogs."

She boldly countered with another saying: "That's true, sir, but even the dogs eat the leftovers that fall from their master's table."

Jesus smiled at her clever reply. "You are a woman of great faith," he beamed. "What you want will be done for you."

Plockhorst

In that moment her daughter was healed.

That night Jesus went out from the house to walk alone under the starry skies. The soft breeze that came up from the seacoast carried the scent of salt.

The disciples stayed at the house and discussed the day's events.

Thaddeus said: "She really was a woman of great faith."

His father James added: "It was like the time the centurion asked Jesus to heal his son."

Peter recalled his own recent, brief walk on the water: "I want to have such strong faith."

"We are with him all the time," Andrew said, "and yet these who are not Jews seem to have a greater faith than we."

Thomas summed it up. "Yes, we praised Jesus in the boat after he walked out to us. She praised Jesus before he healed her daughter."

✞

We are challenged to examine our own faith as we reflect on this Sunday's Gospel. Do you believe in miracles? A Time Magazine poll reported that 69% of Americans said they believed in miracles. Such response is not surprising because most of us have our own miracle story to tell. Miracles surround us. In the Eucharistic the bread and wine become the Body and Blood. In following Jesus, we become his body. More than we know, we are his disciples, struggling as they did, to keep the faith as we continue our journey of life.

21st Sunday in Ordinary Time
Matthew 16: 13-20

'Who do you say that I am?'

Jesus looked down at the footpath beneath him. He was filled with anxiety because this good brown earth he walked upon would soon end for him. The world in which he lived was going to be taken away from him. Jerusalem waited. As Jesus walked he realized each step north was toward a false safety. As long as he was going north he was away from Jerusalem. But time was running swiftly and the days could now be numbered.

John was at his side and saw the worry on Jesus' face. "What troubles you, Lord?" he asked.

Jesus answered with a brave smile. "The future." he said.

Jesus knew that when they reached the Roman city of Caesarea Philippi they would have to turn back. When they started south Jesus would begin the first steps of his own death march.

Having crossed to the east side of the Sea of Galilee, the long-robed men walked to Bethsaida where Jesus restored the sight of a blind man. Bethsaida had been rebuilt and renamed Julias, the name of Emperor Augustus' daughter. This was a political gesture by Philip the Tetrarch. Philip named his own capitol city Caesarea to honor Rome, but added his own name after it to avoid confusion with Caesarea Maritima on the coast.

When Jesus and the disciples arrived at Caesarea Philippi they were deep in a gentile country. No Jews lived here. Roman banners blew in the wind outside the palace. Helmeted centurions guarded the entry to this remote outpost filled with foreigners who pretended to enjoy the grace of Greece under the watchful eyes of the Empire and the Tetrarchy.

In one of the outlying villages near the river Jesus found a place to retreat. For a time he would give his full attention to deepening the formation of the disciples, preparing them to carry on after him. He began with the question: "Who do people say that I am?"

After they answered incorrectly he asked them directly: "And who do you say that I am?"

Peter told him: "You are the Messiah, the Son of the living God."

Jesus praised him: "Good for you, Simon, son of John." Jesus assured him that such an understanding must have been revealed to him directly "by my Father in heaven."

Jesus placed his hands on Peter's strong shoulders and solemnly entrusted him with the future.

"Peter, you are a rock and on this rock foundation I will build my church."

Peter smiled as Jesus called him by his nickname. Peter means rock. Their faith that Jesus was the Messiah was the cornerstone that would have to support the faith of the disciples for the rest of their lives.

Jesus continued: "...and not even death will ever be able to overcome it. I will give you the keys of the Kingdom of heaven."

The disciples listened intently as they were told that Peter would have the power to bind things and to loose things upon the earth. With these keys to the kingdom Peter would receive the transfer of power.

Peter felt a shiver of fear sweep through him. He was just a fisherman. He knew he didn't have the ability or the strength to achieve such heights. Peter wanted to run; back to his boat, back to Capernaum. But he knew he would never be able to return to his peaceful life as a fisherman. Instead, he stood now before an awesome threshold.

It was merciful that he could not comprehend the immensity of what would follow. Peter was trembling as he heard the sounds of the water gurgling over the rocks in the river. A cool breeze fluttered the leaves of

the trees. In the distance there was the sound of summer thunder. It looked like it was going to rain.

✟

We must also answer Jesus' question: "Who do you say that I am? Our own answer will describe our faith. It will also describe the life we lead in this world and in the next.

22nd Sunday in Ordinary Time
Matthew 16: 21-27

'Whoever loses his life for my sake, will find it.'

During the past weeks, wandering in the north country of Phoenicia and Caesarea Philippi, Jesus experienced the bigger world outside his own Jewish lands of Galilee and Judea. Here he encountered the strange religions and gods of the Greeks, Romans and Syrians. Here Jesus was a stranger so he found it a retreat from the crowds of Jews that pursued him in Galilee. But whatever peace this interlude might have offered was destroyed by the nagging storms that raged in his mind whenever he thought about going to Jerusalem. Jesus knew he was a man with a death sentence upon him and time was fast running out.

On the morning that they were finally leaving to start south again, Jesus called the disciples to him. He wanted them to know that each step he took was a step closer to Jerusalem and the suffering he must endure. A dark anxiety gnawed at him like a hungry beast that wouldn't let go.

He explained: "I must go to Jerusalem and suffer much from the elders, the chief priests and the teachers of the Law. I will be put to death, but three days later I will be raised to life."

Peter studied Jesus intently. He could not understand the statement because Jesus was the Messiah. How could anything bad happen to him? Peter walked up to Jesus. "I need to talk to you alone."

Jesus turned to walk down the path that led to the main road. Close behind, Peter pleaded, "God forbid it, Lord! That must never happen to you."

Jesus whirled around to face him and the rest of the astonished disciples. "Get away from me , Satan," he snarled, pushing Peter away in protest.

Making the decision to go to Jerusalem was difficult enough without Peter trying to talk him out of it.

Philip Poteau

Jesus told Peter that his evil thoughts did not come from God, but from man. To not accept God's plan was the same as an attempt to destroy it.

Then Jesus told the disciples that if they wanted to follow him they would have to quit thinking about themselves and take up their crosses. Then he said: "Whoever wants to save his own life will lose it; but whoever loses his life for my sake will find it."

They all stood in silence, thinking about what he had just said to them. Jesus turned and began to march resolutely down the road that he would follow all the way to Jerusalem. Peter watched him for a moment, then hurried after. The rest of the disciples soon followed.

The Gospel invites us to pick up our own cross each day and follow Jesus. We are told that by living a selfish life on our terms we will lose the life that God would give us. We are told that following Jesus can cost us our imagined life; but if we have the courage to follow him anyway, we will receive the real life he offers along with his rewards for our good deeds.

23rd Sunday in Ordinary Time
Matthew 18: 15-20

Where two or three are gathered...

Jesus and his disciples had climbed up a quiet hillside to a flat spot from which they could look back down on the city of Capernaum. Farther up was a grove of trees, but the afternoon was cool so they sat and warmed themselves under the bright sun.

Gathered in a circle, they sat facing each other. Since Peter and Andrew had gotten into a little squabble, Jesus was talking to them about brothers fighting against each other.

Peter and his brother Andrew looked glumly across the circle at the other pair of brothers, James and John. All four of them were recalling the many times that they had quarreled. Jesus smiled at them as he settled back on the grass to share his teaching.

"If your brother should commit some wrong against you," Jesus said, "go and point out his fault, but keep it between the two of you." Jesus watched them earnestly. No-one said anything so Jesus continued.

"If he listens to you, you have won your brother over."

Thomas seemed smug without having a brother present, so he posed the inevitable question.

"What if he doesn't listen?" Thomas asked.

Jesus was quick with his reply.

"If he doesn't listen, summon another, so that every case may stand on the word of two or three witnesses."

The disciples continued their exchange of "what-if" questions until they expanded to include the entire church.

"And," one of them said, "what if the brother ignores even the church? What then?"

"Treat him as you would a Gentile or a tax collector," Jesus directed.

He went on to reassure them with the words he had previously spoken to Simon Peter.

"Whatever you declare bound on earth will be bound in heaven, and whatever you declare loosed on earth shall be held loosed in heaven."

Just then a flock of birds flashed overhead, disappearing into the grove of trees higher up. The distraction made the disciples fall silent, leaving each with his own thoughts amid the beauty and peacefulness of the place.

Later the disciples began to wonder about how things would be after Jesus was gone. They asked many questions, thinking up all possible situations. To end their anxiety, Jesus assured them that even if he were physically absent he would still be with them.

"Again I tell you," he said, "if two of you join your voices on earth to pray for anything whatever, it shall be granted you by my Father in heaven. Where two or three are gathered in my name, there am I in their midst."

✝

The Gospel reminds us that whenever we gather in Jesus name, he is there! We find him in our Sunday celebration. We find him in our prayer around the family table. We also find him powerfully present in small faith-sharing and Bible study groups. Because he lives in each of us, we see him reflected in the eyes of one another.

24th Sunday in Ordinary Time
Matthew 18: 21-35

Seventy times seven!

Peter started the whole thing when he asked Jesus how many times he would have to forgive his brother for sinning against him. Peter was hoping to get a clear response—a nice, easy rule. A number. Peter was hoping to hear a limit.

"Seven times?" Peter asked hopefully.

Jesus' answered, "Seventy times seven!"

Peter almost gasped. This meant there was practically no limit. Peter shrugged and threw his hands up in a gesture of hopelessness. He could never forgive that many times!

Jesus began to tell them a story about a king who discovered his servant had stolen a huge sum of money. When the servant asked for mercy the king forgave the servant and the debt.

The disciples were surprised at the king's generosity. Jesus continued with what was going to be one of the sternest lessons Peter and the disciples would ever receive. When that forgiven servant in the story failed to forgive someone who owed him money the king learned of it. Angered that the servant had not shown the same mercy he had been given, the king handed him over to the torturers and made him repay his huge debt.

The Disciples had no trouble reading the moral of the story. God forgives those who forgive others.

Matthew pressed his fingers against his forehead to ease the headache that Jesus was giving him. His years as a public tax collector had taught him to collect debts, not forgive them.

"This king in the story," Matthew argued, "is unlike any kings of this world. The servant was guilty of stealing. He should have been punished. I can't believe that any king would feel sorry for him and forgive the debt."

Jesus smiled back at Matthew and looked peacefully at his other wondering disciples. Thomas, seeing a deeper meaning to the story, reminded Matthew of a point: "Jesus said that the kingdom of God was like that. Perhaps the king is like God himself." Thomas glanced at Jesus for approval.

John added his insight: "We are like the servant of the king. If we don't forgive debts that are owed to us, we can't expect God to forgive us our debts."

Peter saw the darker side of the parable, recalling: "Yes, but don't forget, when the servant failed to forgive his debtors the king no longer forgave the servant. He went to prison to be punished until he paid his huge debt back."

Silence settled over the group. Bartholomew pulled some bread from his sack and tore off a small piece. He started to eat it, then briefly offered some to Philip who was sitting next to him. Philip waved the bread away. Bartholomew stuffed it into his mouth and thoughtfully began to chew. Jesus seemed pleased that the message was being learned.

When no one spoke for a long time, Jesus issued a final warning. His face hardened as he spoke.

"My heavenly Father will treat you in exactly the same way unless each of you forgives his brother from his heart."

✟

The Gospel parable invites us to search for the people in our lives who we have not forgiven. Most of us have been deeply hurt in the past. Some of us have been able to forgive. Others may still be carrying bitterness. We cannot track the clean floors of heaven with the muddy boots of our resentments. We must first clean away all anger by forgiving everyone who has offended us. It is a stern lesson indeed. It's a lesson we need to remember each time we pray the Lord's Prayer: "...forgive us our trespasses as we forgive those who trespass against us."

25th Sunday in Ordinary Time
Matthew 20: 1-16

Those who are last, will be first!

The disciples were down by the lake with Jesus and the afternoon's discussion was full of revelation. Jesus had just told them that they would one day sit on thrones to rule the twelve tribes of Israel. He promised eternal life but warned that many that are now first, will be last; and many that are now last will be first.

Thaddeus asked Jesus: "How can those who are now last, be the first? What about those of us who have followed you from the very beginning? Surely we, who were the first, will always be so honored."

Thomas started to join Thaddeus in his argument, but a dark realization stopped him. It suddenly occurred to him that his own faith could be lost, his own promises might be broken. Things are not always the same. People change for better or for worse.

Jesus tossed a pebble out onto the water and watched the wave rings widen. The rings spread from the center where the pebble had broken the water's surface. The rings were like his idea which was widening and growing. Jesus turned back to his group and sat down on the ground, preparing to tell them a story. He leaned back against a tree.

"The Kingdom of Heaven is like this," Jesus began. "Once there was a man who went out early in the morning to hire some men to work in his vineyard…"

When Jesus ended the story he emphasized that the employer's generosity was like that of God. He went on to clarify: "…those who are last will be first and those who are first will be last."

The disciples were fascinated by the strange twist of Jesus' clever tale—all except Thaddeus who was still struggling with the concept. Eventually the rings of understanding would encircle him and he too would know the wisdom that God's ways are not the ways of men. All of the disciples would realize that everyone is called to unselfishly rejoice in God's wonderful generosity to his creation.

✞

The parable of the vineyard workers teaches the lesson that all we really have is God's generosity. If we really got what we deserve we might not be such sticklers for justice. It might be a much different story. There is really nothing we can do to "deserve" eternal life or any other gift from God. All we can do is stand in wonder as God patiently forgives us for our weakness, loves us anyway, and still surrounds us with the gifts from his immense generosity.

26th Sunday in Ordinary Time
Matthew 21: 28-32

Repent, and believe in him!

The late afternoon shadow of the Synagogue building had already crept across the gardens, reaching the low rock wall that formed the courtyard. On the other side of the wall was the road which led south toward Jerusalem. A man leading three camels floated past. He was probably going to load them for a caravan to Damascus. Other merchants and tradesmen were also hurrying along the road.

In the Synagogue courtyard, Jesus and some of the disciples were engaged in a debate with the elders and the chief priests.

One aging priest pointed his withered finger at Jesus: "I have heard the stories about you."

Jesus responded, "And I have asked that they not be told."

"You have spoken to the wind. Why have you done your deeds for the gentiles? Why have you taken meals with prostitutes and tax collectors? Are you not a Jew like us?" The priest's flurry of questions left him gasping for air.

Peter was getting irritated. These elders and priests were just trying to make Jesus look bad. Peter rose, his deep voice growling the words: "Jesus fed five thousand Jews a few weeks ago!"

The priest's charge reminded Jesus of the Samaritan woman at the well and the Syro-Phoenecian woman who had followed him all the way to Tyre. Jesus wanted to respond directly that the gentiles seemed to believe in him, but most of the Jews were skeptical. He decided it would be better to teach with a parable.

"What do you think of this case?" Jesus began. "There was a man who had two sons..."

Jesus related the story of how the first son promised to go to work, but didn't. The second son rebelled against the father's authority and refused to go. But later the second son regretted what he had said and decided to go to the vineyard to work.

The elders pulled at their beards and reflected on the parable.

Then Jesus said: "Let me make it clear that tax collectors and prostitutes are entering the kingdom of God before you."

Peter smirked at Jesus bold conclusion, glancing at the priests and elders who were glaring angrily back at the youthful Jesus before them. Jesus stabbed the air with his finger and charged on: "When John came preaching a way of holiness, you put no faith in him; but the tax collectors and the prostitutes did believe in him. Yet even when you saw that, you did not repent and believe in him!"

✞

The parable provides a little mirror through which we can see our true selves. On Sunday we may be like the first son who says, "Yes Lord, I am going to follow you and serve you." But then comes Monday and we may fail to do it. At other times we may be the rebellious second son, refusing to do what we know God is calling us to do.

When we do decide to obey the commandments which the Father has given us...when we do decide to follow Jesus...when with the help of the Holy Spirit we faithfully live up to those commitments, then will our actions have met the parable's test of obedience.

Plockhorst

7th Sunday in Ordinary Time
Matthew 21: 33-43

Grapes of wrath!

The leafy trees at the edge of the vineyard provided cool shade for Jesus and the disciples. By the generosity of the owner of the vineyard, this would be the site of their encampment for the night.

The vineyard owner was a proud little man, happily chattering about the fine wine that came from his robust grapes. He marched up between the rows of vines and then turned to face his guests. The vines were fat with dark-red grapes that had ripened in the warm Galilean sun. The owner parted some leaves with his hand and quickly found a clump of big grapes, offering them to Jesus.

"Try some," he beamed, "they're the very best I have ever grown."

Jesus sampled a grape, then ate the entire clump. "Delicious!" he said.

That evening, after the harvesters had deserted the hillside, in a pale dawning, the full moon began to rise. Jesus and his men sat alone by the vineyard, beneath the dark trees. Silence settled over them like a warm blanket. Peter was already sound asleep, one hand resting atop a belly full of wine, which the kind vintner had provided.

John and Andrew sat down next to Jesus, who seemed deep in thought as he stared at the moonlit vineyard. Jesus smiled at the two: "I was thinking about another parable," he told them. "Tomorrow I will tell it to the chief priests and the elders."

"Tell us tonight," Andrew asked.

Jesus chuckled at Andrew's eagerness, giving him the outline. "It's about the man who planted a fine vineyard, leaving it in the care of tenant farmers. At the harvest the landowner sent three of his slaves to collect his share. The farmers killed one and beat and stoned the other two. He sent more slaves who where also dispelled. Then the owner sent his son who they killed. The farmers now had to face the wrath of the owner himself."

"Why did they kill the son?" Andrew asked.

Jesus explained that Jewish law would allow the farmers to inherit the land if there was no heir to it. He then quoted the scripture about the stone, which the builders had at first rejected which later became the cornerstone of the building. Jesus' mind stayed on that thought. He was that cornerstone, rejected by the elders and chief priests of his day, but was already becoming the foundation of new faith.

Peter began to snore. Andrew grinned, "Sounds like he has the right idea." John yawned and began to spread his robes beneath him. Jesus gathered his robes around himself and leaned back. It was getting late. Suddenly, Jesus propped himself up on one elbow and added the last bit to his story: "For this reason, I tell you, the kingdom of God will be taken away from you and given to a people that will yield a rich harvest."

✝

This parable warns us that the kingdom of God can be taken away from us if we do not produce a rich harvest in our lives. God has indeed prepared a beautiful vineyard for us. We are temporary farmers, living our lives on God's green earth. In the past five Sundays we have heard parables which taught us to take up our cross and follow him; to humbly correct the faults of others; to forgive others; to be content; and to obey. If we reject these teachings, then we are rejecting the cornerstone, Jesus himself. And without Jesus we can have no harvest.

Plockhorst

28th Sunday in Ordinary Time
Matthew 22: 1-14

The wedding feast

The wedding banquet was a pleasant surprise for Jesus and the disciples. A royal messenger had come out to them as they were walking on the Jerusalem road. "Stop," he had called. "Follow me, you are all invited to the royal wedding feast at the villa on the hilltop." His arm directed their vision to the white-walled buildings surrounded by narrow spears of cypress trees.

Assured that there was much to eat and drink, the disciples followed the messenger to the gates of the villa. As they drew closer they heard the music and singing. The large courtyard had been decorated with banners honoring the young prince and his bride. Tables were piled high with roasted meat and fancy dishes of vegetables, breads and dates and fruits. They began to enjoy, especially Peter who was waving his quickly emptied wine cup with his left hand while hungrily stuffing pieces of lamb in his mouth with the other hand.

Jesus noted that the food preparations for the wedding banquet greatly exceeded the number of people who were there.

"Where are all the other guests?" Jesus asked the servant who was pouring him a cup of wine. The server, speaking softly, told Jesus that the invited guests had refused to come. Some of the royal messengers sent to invite them had been driven off. A few messengers, those who failed to return, might have been killed.

By evening the royal messengers had rounded up hundreds of people who now filled the villa. The music, the food, the wine, the loud talk and laughter lasted far into the night. When Peter surfaced some hours later, his face was much redder. His wine cup was empty again. With slightly drooping eyelids, Peter gazed lovingly at Jesus. Showing him his empty cup, Peter announced: "I think they have run out of wine."

Jesus smiled back tolerantly, remembering another wedding years ago in Cana when his mother had spoken those same words to him.

That night, just before dropping off to sleep, Jesus meditated on the day's events. He suddenly realized how much this wedding banquet was like God's invitation to his people. He saw clearly how the people reject God's invitation. It was clear that those who reject God will learn too late what a tragic mistake they have made.

✠

This parable can teach us that the kingdom which God offers us is very much like a sumptuous wedding feast. How could we ever be too busy to attend? How could we ever send God's messengers away, refusing to even hear his word; refusing to partake in his Eucharist? Perhaps we should examine our response to God. We are invited in so many ways. Each day invites us to deepen our faith and understanding of it. Sunday mass invites us to attend the banquet of God.

29th Sunday in Ordinary Time
Matthew 22: 15-21

Caesar's coin!

"There he is, over there, under the tree," one of the four stern-faced Pharisees said as they emerged from the synagogue. The bright afternoon sun made them squint to see Jesus and two of his disciples resting in the shade. These Pharisees were the local wise men, devout members of the strictest sect of Jews. They lived every letter of the Mosaic Law and hoped for the day when Israel would be God's nation again, free of the Romans and Herod.

Jesus glanced up at the four men squinting at him. They turned away quickly when they saw him looking back. The Pharisees sauntered across the temple courtyard toward another group, which was also eyeing Jesus.

"I think this is a good time for our little question," the black-bearded Pharisee smirked.

"Even we followers of Herod would agree with that," one from the other group said.

It was an unusual alliance. Herod's men said Jesus was a threat to their money and power if he really was a king or the Messiah. The Pharisees said God was the true ruler of Israel and paying tax to Rome denied God.

When they drew close, one of the Pharisees told the group around him, "It is a most cleverly contrived question."

The black-bearded one said: "If Jesus says not to pay the tax to the Emperor he could be arrested by Roman authorities. If he says to pay the tax, he will mark himself as a traitor to God."

"It's still early," one suggested. Let's wait until more people are here to watch him put his foot in his own mouth." The Pharisees and the Herodians drifted like a school of hungry fish. More people arrived.

"Either way, by sundown Jesus will no longer be a problem here," a Herodian snarled, glancing quickly at his victim.

"Sabbath greetings," Thaddeus said as he joined Jesus, Andrew and John. "I saw the others coming just behind me."

The sun was slowly landing behind the western hills when the black-bearded Pharisee stepped up onto the stone ledge surrounding the courtyard. He shouted for all to hear. "I have a question for the Teacher."

Turning to Jesus, the Pharisee paused for dramatic effect, waiting until everyone grew quiet. "Teacher, we know you are a truthful man and teach God's way sincerely. You court no one's favor and do not act out of human respect. Give us your opinion, then, in this case. Is it lawful to pay tax to the emperor or not?"

Jesus rose to his feet like a gathering storm cloud and threw his arms skyward. Sparks of light seemed to bristle in his eyes at the outrage of their trickery.

"Why are you trying to trip me up, you hypocrites?" Jesus thundered.

The little band of Pharisees and Herodians seemed to shrink together, fearful of Jesus' stormy response.

Stalking toward them Jesus demanded, "Show me the coin used for the tax."

Blackbeard fumbled in his robe and produced a silver denarius. Jesus took the coin and held it between his thumb and forefinger, turning to show the face of it to all the crowd.

"Whose head is this and whose inscription?" Jesus asked of them.

"Caesar's," came the reply.

Knowing the power of what he was about to say, Jesus smiled in spite of himself.

"Then give to Caesar what is Caesar's, but give to God what is God's."

✟

If we can't serve two masters, who is our one master? Is it this little world and this little moment in time we call our life? Or is our one master the creator of all the worlds and all the universes; the one who walks among the stars and down the timeless corridors of eternity? Is it his image that is inscribed in our heart?

30th Sunday in Ordinary Time
Matthew 22:34-40

The greatest of these is love

The Pharisee with the thick black beard was probably the most skillful lawyer in all Jerusalem. As a devout follower of the Mosaic Law, he had studied all 613 Jewish commandments, plus all 365 prohibitions and each of the 248 ordinances. In debate he never lost. The only dark shadows on his brilliance were his recent encounters with Jesus. His well crafted, seemingly "no-win" questions had only served to give Jesus a fresh opportunity to enthrall new followers.

Today it was going to be different! The entire assembly of Pharisees was present outside the synagogue to watch Jesus fall into their trap. The black beard lawyer, standing in the midst of his brethren, seemed jubilant.

Across the courtyard the sunlight exploded against Jesus' white robe. His back was turned to the Pharisees while he taught those seated at his feet. Their questions came at random. Jesus answered, sometimes with a parable story, sometimes with a thought-provoking return question. Sometimes Jesus would give a direct answer.

The Pharisees were talking among themselves when the one with the black beard suddenly shouted his question over to Jesus.

His loud voice split the air, silencing everyone. "Teacher, which commandment of the law is the greatest?"

The question floated out like bait on a hook. The black bearded Pharisee waited hopefully for Jesus to strike.

Jesus first response ignored the bait. It was a quote directly from the Book of Deuteronomy, the Shema, the Jewish profession of faith: "You shall love your God with your whole heart, with your whole soul, and with all your mind."

The Pharisee swallowed.

Jesus continued, "This is the greatest and first commandment." Then, recalling a passage from the Book of Leviticus, Jesus continued. "The second is like it: 'You shall love your neighbor as yourself.' On these two commandments the whole law is based, and the prophets as well."

The two opposing clusters of men were silent. Their own laws called them not to quarrel, but to actually love one another. Jesus' answer left them speechless.

✟

Time and again Jesus calls us to love one another. It is the Commandment that heals every heart. If we follow it, our days are filled with joy. As Paul reminds us, "There are in the end three things that last: faith, hope, and love, and the greatest of these is love."

31st Sunday in Ordinary Time
Matthew 23: 1-12

The greatest among you must be your servant!

The old Pharisee smiled smugly to himself as he carefully rolled the strips of parchment. Written upon the strips were quotations from the Hebrew scripture. He then placed these holy papers inside the black Phylactery boxes. It was the ritual that preceded morning and evening prayers at the synagogue.

The graying, old rabbi then proceeded to tie one of the boxes to his left wrist and the other was strapped around his forehead. By doing this, these words would remain on his mind and in his work. The wide boxes tied to him were also an outward sign that this rabbi was a very holy man.

Jesus saw it differently. After morning prayers, the rabbi emerged from the synagogue, moving slowly, still wearing his Phylactery boxes and an extravagant blue and white woven tassel. Jesus watched him thoughtfully. Then, turning to the disciples and the crowd around him, he spoke out: "The scribes and the Pharisees have succeeded Moses as teachers; therefore, do everything and observe everything they tell you. But do not follow their example. Their words are bold, but their deeds are few."

Jesus went on to comment how these rabbis made great demands of others, yet did no work themselves.

Jesus pointed at the rabbi walking past. "All their works are performed to be seen. They widen their phylacteries and wear huge tassels. They are fond of places of honor at banquets and the front seats in synagogues, of marks of respect in public and of being called rabbi."

The old Pharisee stopped for a moment and glared angrily at Jesus. When he walked on, Jesus returned his attention to the crowd around him.

"As to you, avoid the title 'Rabbi.' One among you is your teacher, the rest are learners. Do not call anyone on earth your father. Only one is your father, the One in heaven."

Jesus explained again that they should avoid being called teachers because only the Messiah was their true teacher.

It was nearly mid-day, so Jesus rose to leave them and return to the house where he was staying. Before departing, he left them with a final thought: "The greatest among you will be the one who serves the rest. Whoever exalts himself shall be humbled, but whoever humbles himself shall be exalted."

✟

The lesson Jesus gives us in the Gospel this week may seem to point to churchmen and women who enjoy their vestments and titles more than they enjoy good works. But the Gospel really speaks to all of us Christians who "wear" our religion as a way of making ourselves look good. We are thus reminded that our God sees who we really are. Realizing that, we can more easily humble ourselves and become the ones who serve the rest.

32nd Sunday in Ordinary Time
Matthew 25: 1-13

Five torches

The loud voices coming down the road woke them. It sounded like a large group of men, laughing and singing as they approached. Jesus and the disciples were sprawled in slumber beneath a canopy of olive trees near the road.

Jesus opened his eyes to the darkness. John, nearby, was already sitting up. "Sounds like a wedding party," he said.

"So late?" Jesus asked. "Half the night is already gone!" Jesus rolled onto his right side and pulled his robe tighter around his neck. He tried to drift back to sleep as the noisy group faded down the roadway toward the bride's house.

In wedding celebrations the groom and his friends go to the home of the bride to claim her. Her bridesmaids come out to meet the men and by torchlight lead them to the home of the bride. Then, with her bridesmaids and family around her, the entire procession returns to the home of the groom for the rest of the all-night celebration. Even as he fell asleep, Jesus knew it would not be long before the larger wedding procession would be returning down the road.

The clang of tambourines and singing women came in what seemed an eyeblink. Jesus decided to get to his feet and watch. He counted five torches blazing in the night. The bridesmaids held their torches high, lighting the roadway for the procession. But, the custom called for ten bridesmaids. As the party passed, Jesus wondered, "Where are the other five bridesmaids?"

Jesus sat for awhile, imagining that the other five bridesmaids had run out of oil. They were no doubt desperately trying to get some at this late hour. They were going to miss the festive singing and dancing and the moment when the bride was brought into the groom's home under the wedding canopy. They would miss the celebration that they had been looking forward to for weeks. If they didn't get oil and catch up with the procession they would never be admitted once the gates to the groom's home were locked for the night. If only they had been prepared.

Jesus knew it would be a powerful parable story to tell the disciples. It was a good teaching story to let everyone understand that they must be prepared. To receive the Kingdom of God, they must make a choice and follow it now.

When the disciples gathered with him at daybreak, Jesus began to teach them. He said: "The reign of God can be likened to ten bridesmaids who took their torches and went out to welcome the groom..."

✟

Some say Jesus is the groom and we are the bridesmaids. Some of us are prepared to meet him when he comes. Others, maybe not. The lesson of the parable is to make sure we are prepared for our eventual encounter with Jesus. That preparation must be by our possession of the oil of faith and how brightly we keep it burning in our lives.

33rd Sunday in Ordinary Time
Matthew 25: 14:30

Day of reckoning

The friends of Jesus sometimes offered him a little money to help out with his ministry. Those who were grateful for his healings, also gave gifts. This money was used by Jesus to buy food and sometimes lodging for himself and his disciples. These coins were carried in a goatskin bag which one of the disciples kept. Usually the treasurer was Matthew because, as a former tax collector, he had always handled money. But sometimes Peter carried the coins because he was the biggest and the strongest and frequently took charge of things.

It was Peter who lost the money. With his empty hands held up in supplication, Peter tried to explain: "The coin bag was inside my bundle. I usually tie it to my belt. It must have fallen out along the road somewhere..."

The other disciples were not consoled with Peter's words. Without money they could buy no food. Young Thaddeus turned and stalked away, stabbing the ground with his walking stick.

Jesus watched silently, remembering a parable about stewardship and responsibility. Peter had been responsible for their money and had lost it all. The parable told the story of three men who were responsible for their employer's money when he left to take a long trip.

But this incident with Peter put more at stake than a few lost coins. It was a moment that could cost the disciples their unity. It was really a question of continuing together and living lives of love and forgiveness.

Jesus spoke: "My brothers, we must all love each other. Don't be angry with Peter. Peter has only lost some coins. Each of us stands to lose much more if we are not responsible for the greater gift of caring for each other. Each one of you carries a treasure from my Father. Don't lose that treasure today."

Jesus then began to tell the parable. He told how two of the men doubled their employer's money. But the third employee, who was fearful, buried the money in a field to keep it safe. On the day of reckoning, when the employer returned from his long journey, he praised the two who doubled his money. When the third returned only the original silver, his employer grew angry.

Jesus concluded. "Yield a harvest in your lives. Return more than what you have been given."

The tension over the lost money eased a little as each thought about the story.

This parable comes down like a fence around each of our lives. Inside that fence we find the ground that is ours. We are in the center of that ground, alone with our life as we have lived it. On our day of reckoning we will be asked: What have we done with our lives? Have we invested our God-given talents wisely? Have we been able to double the gifts that we have been given? Or have we wasted our lives, doing nothing, burying our talent in the ground?

Christ the King Sunday
Matthew 25: 31:46

The last judgment

The top of the hill above Bethany gave a good view of the Jericho Road which wandered east, down to the Jordan Valley. The hilltop also received the scented afternoon wind which blew through the markets of Jerusalem, vaulted the Kidron Valley and rustled through the olive trees on the western slopes of Gethsemane. John's hair danced around his face as the breeze cooled him. He watched Jesus as he left the group, walking alone down the hillside path to Bethany.

Jesus had just told his disciples a powerful story describing what will happen when the Son of Man comes in his glory, escorted by all the angels in heaven.

"We should remember this story to tell to others." John said.

James raised his eyebrows in agreement. "You should remember it to remind yourself to love others. I'll remember it because I want the blessing of the Father. I want to inherit the kingdom he has prepared for me."

Peter grinned: "Then what must you do, James? What is it that Jesus wants you to do?"

"Well, Jesus said that as often as we help others we help him."

Simon joined in, "Yes, to love one another."

"Even lepers?" Thomas asked.

"Especially lepers," John said, glancing at the now empty path where Jesus had walked. A memory flashed in his head—the day he had seen Jesus make ten lepers clean. "It is always the poor, the sick, the lame, the lepers, even Samaritans. These are the people Jesus has loved."

"Herod doesn't need our love, he has his gold." Matthew said.

James disagreed. "Jesus' story says what ever you do to the least of his brothers you do to him. Everyone is our brother, from the poorest to the richest. Even Pilate, even Caesar. Are we not all brothers in the Father's family?"

Peter growled at the prospect of loving Caesar. "We've enough people to love just among us Jews. Let's not take on the whole world just yet. We can love Rome later."

The conversation continued as the disciples went single-file down the path to rejoin Jesus in the village of Bethany. Two days later Jesus would enter Jerusalem for the last time.

✞

Peter did not know then that he would one day carry the love of Jesus all the way to Rome. He would die doing it, being crucified upside down. His last vision would be of Caesar's city where one day a great basilica would be built, a church bearing his name, a church with a message of love that would spread around the world. We do not know what we will encounter in our lives. We only know that like Jesus, we are called to love one another. In that love we find life. Without it, we perish.

The Gospel Stories of Jesus is available on a CD

To facilitate the insertion of each weekly Gospel story into your church Sunday bulletin, or other program, this book has been downloaded onto a CD. You will find a folder for each week. In each folder is a text file, the illustration file and a Portable Document File of that week's story. The PDF shows you a single page layout with suggested type formatting. These single sheet stories can be printed directly from your computer and make ideal handouts for bible study and other groups.

The story is in rich text format and the accompanying illustration is stored as a jpeg. This will enable you to flow the text into your particular layout. Apply your own style of text formatting. You can also size the illustration to fit your space.

Insert the CD in your computer, scroll to the current week and highlight the story. Then just copy and paste. The same procedure applies for the illustration.

Here's how to order your CD version:

To order by mail

Send your mailing address and check (payable to Deacon Dick Folger) for $7.95 to
The Gospel Stories of Jesus
32026 Trevor Avenue
Hayward, California 94544

To order by phone

Call Deacon Dick Folger direct
at 510-475-7669.

To order via the internet

e-mail dickfolger@aol.com

Please include the following information:
• Ship to address
• Authorization to charge your credit card for $7.95.
• Include credit card number and expiration.

Your order will be sent, postage paid to you by U.S. Mail.